# Praise for *No M*

C000156677

"Heather Hiscox critiques the
urges changemakers to deep
tion with the people they support. This book will nudge you
to think more critically about how you work and will provide
you with an excellent roadmap for exploring ideas that could
lead to long-lasting social change."

**DR. LESLEY-ANN NOEL**, co-editor, *The Black Experience
in Design*; creator, The Designer's Critical Alphabet and
Positionality Wheel

"*No More Status Quo* is a candid interrogation of approaches that
aren't working and offers solutions that are practical and road-
tested. Heather Hiscox weaves in her own experiences with
expert insights to show how we can disrupt our current ways
of changemaking to bring about more sustained impact."

**NATE WONG**, partner at The Bridgespan Group; former
chief strategy and innovation officer at the Beeck Center for
Social Impact and Innovation, Georgetown University

"A must-read for nonprofit leaders looking to innovate faster
and increase their impact. Heather Hiscox's stakeholder-
centric approach provides a proven framework for reducing
the uncertainty associated with change, driving down waste,
and increasing meaningful impact."

**GABE COOPER**, CEO, Virtuous Software

"Heather Hiscox brings the 'lean start-up' approach into the
2020s. With a sense of humility and a social justice perspective, Hiscox offers all nonprofit leaders the resources we need
to pause—so that we can speed up social change!"

**RUSTY STAHL**, founder, president and CEO, Fund the People

No More
Status Quo

# A Proven Framework to Change the Way We Change the World

# NO MORE STATUS QUO

## HEATHER HISCOX

Cataloguing in publication information is available from Library and Archives Canada.
ISBN 978-1-77458-253-4 (paperback)
ISBN 978-1-77458-254-1 (ebook)
ISBN 978-1-77458-318-0 (audiobook)

Page Two
pagetwo.com

Edited by Emily Schultz
Copyedited by Steph VanderMeulen
Cover and interior design by Taysia Louie

23 24 25 26 27  5 4 3 2 1


PauseforChange.com
NoMoreStatusQuoBook.com

# Contents

# ONE

## WHAT'S DYSFUNCTIONAL ABOUT STATUS QUO PROBLEM-SOLVING?

# Calling All Frustrated Changemakers

DEAR FRUSTRATED Changemaker,
  This book is for you. Honestly, it's the book I wish I had many years ago. I use the word "frustrated" because that was who I was and still am working as a changemaker in the social impact sector. And just so we are on the same page, when I use the term "social impact sector," or "social sector" or "the sector" for short, I am talking about and include what I call the intersection or triad of social change—nonprofit, local government, and philanthropy. While many of the challenges I discuss are not exclusively unique to the social sector, the skills and stories I share were molded by my work in social change.

  Since I was old enough to form the words, when I was asked what I wanted to do when I grew up, I answered, "Change the world." It has been really hard to feel so frustrated, to feel like I am the only person who sees the harm of status quo problem-solving, and who is searching for new ways to do this sacred work.

  I used to play by the "rules" and norms and felt disappointed and disillusioned. I used to wonder if our programs really made significant changes in people's lives. I used to question how we were supposed to engage in meaningful work when we were chasing one meeting, partner, and grant to the next. I used to look at community members whom we were so blessed to support and see how often they were ignored and left out. I saw too many leaders and organizations jumping to solutions and wasting resources without a process to guide their decision-making.

Any of this sound familiar?

What I've come to know and what drives my work is that *status quo problem-solving skills in the social impact sector are creating weak impact and waste at scale.*

This book is dedicated to unpacking this one statement and showing how you can work differently to address uncertainty and create deeper impact, all while using less time and fewer resources. We really can change the way we change the world.

I know now that I am one of many frustrated changemakers who are just like you, working through very real struggles, ready for no more status quo. I hope this book gives you support and the belief that you can use new skills to drive change in your organization and community.

I am continually inspired by these words from Maya Angelou: "Do the best you can until you know better. Then when you know better, do better." Together, we are on a learning journey, and we can learn and do better for ourselves and our sector. Thank you for being open to learning all the ways you can impact the world every day.

## Why I'm Writing This Book Now

The first reason now is the moment for this book is that I am finally answering a call for support. At nearly every speaking engagement I've had, an audience member has asked, "Is there something I can read to learn more about this framework?" Before now, the only answer was no, unless you wanted to hire my firm to work one-on-one with your organization. It is time for this framework to reach more people, and more organizations, for whom this way of thinking is new and very much needed.

These new types of problem-solving skills, which are not typically used in the sector, used to be totally new to me too. I didn't know it ten years ago, but what I was looking for was something to help me navigate the uncertainty and overwhelm interwoven into the sector. Sure, I could have just ignored those pesky feelings, and maybe rocked back and forth under my desk repeating "capitalism, racism, patriarchy," but instead I lifted my head and explored new perspectives, guides, and possibilities.

My exploration began when I entered the start-up scene. Before I immersed myself in start-up culture, I had never heard of the Business Model Canvas, Lean Canvas, Human-Centered Design, Design Thinking, or Lean Experimentation. I entered the space as a total outsider. I was a thirty-something mom with young babies, focused not on tech or an app but on how to change the world. I embraced challenging the typical image of an entrepreneur, and within just a few years, I launched a local online matchmaking service for nonprofits and the community to share their unused goods. I also wrote a weekly column sharing the ongoing needs of local nonprofits for five years, taught lean innovation to local social impact start-ups, and cofounded the social impact arm of a global consulting firm.

I went from not knowing who Steve Blank, Eric Ries, or Alex Osterwalder were to having dinner at Steve's house as part of the Lean Innovation Educators Summit (my favorite moment: when I told Steve that I was using lean innovation for social good and he told me, "You are the most important person in this room"), exploring with Ann Mei Chang in the early days as she was writing *Lean Impact* whether we should write the book together, and investigating how to scale what is now a national social impact accelerator.

While I loved seeing how start-up methodologies brought people to life, how new actions connected teams more deeply to their customers and to each other, and how rapidly they gathered insights to disrupt their assumptions and inform their decision-making, I started to realize that the start-up world and these methodologies were insufficient for creating social impact and social good. None of these start-up and design methods were initially created for social change and social justice.

These methods can also feel overwhelming, overbuilt, and exclusive. Amelia Klawon, with whom I launched two business ventures, shared my passion for figuring out how to challenge the status quo. From 2015 to 2020, we committed to designing a framework that was easy to use, streamlined, and impactful. We would learn about a method, try it out, find gaps for social impact, and experiment with ways to address what was missing. When Amelia stepped away in June 2020 to do fantastic work in her local community, I took sole ownership of the company and embraced a period of deep introspection, analysis, and expansion.

I took what we created and rooted the framework more deeply in social justice and committed to assessing every component of the content (literally every slide and talking point) from an accessibility and equity lens. Is it perfect? Nope. Is it ever-evolving? Yep. The skills themselves were born from questioning, challenging, and iterating, and I am committed to continuing to "eat my own dog food." The framework is alive and adaptive and is nourished and strengthened by what I learn from and with amazing people just like you.

The second reason I wanted to bring this book to life now is that I have never seen a time as ripe as now for change. While I have been disappointed in what we settle for and call "impact" for many years, COVID-19 and the rise in racial justice movements have jarred our sector as a whole out of complacency. I feel we are finally now asking bigger questions and calling for accountability and more meaningful action sector-wide.

Since most of my professional career has been tied in some way to the social sector, and I'm guessing yours has intertwined as well, you might be able to relate to some of my frustrations. When I worked in program design, I wondered why we were waiting for a "final," "perfect," "ta-da" reveal of our solution when we didn't know if it would even work. When I worked in fundraising, I did not understand why we had to pander to wealthy, older, white men, often whose only claim to fame was being born and who cared more about wielding power than about our mission. When I worked in grant writing, I wondered how in the heck we would pull off the outsized expectations of impact required in lengthy grant applications with only a pittance of funding. I have so many more examples of frustration that include elements of strategic planning, event design, evaluation, pitch competitions, and change management, and I'm sure you have your own to add to the list!

Specifically, these struggles have shown up for me and my clients in ways such as

- being asked to execute a solution that feels like it was created in a vacuum, distant from those most impacted;

- struggling to communicate with decision-makers about which solutions to pursue;

- feeling like we are supposed to have the clear answer, even when the true problem is murky;

- becoming frozen due to the many possibilities available or stakeholders involved;

- investing energy in a solution that seems like it should work, only to have it disappoint; and

- trying to meet the urgency of the need but losing impact in the speed.

While we are talking about these dysfunctions and disappointments, we are also talking about what could be reimagined, and that gives me hope. I'm seeing what used to be talked about only in restaurant booths (way in the back with no one around) finally being discussed in full ballrooms and Zoom rooms. We are acknowledging out loud that the very foundation and construction of the social sector, the structures, processes, and "best practices," are flawed and skewed to favor power and privilege. We are recognizing that the sector roots that are in some places tangled, rotten, and destructive must be exposed and transplanted in new visions, practices, and skills to create new outcomes.

So much of what we accept as true, "the way" to do things, or something that cannot be changed *is absolutely up to us to change*. Our past and existing policies and practices did not arrive from "on high" or on chiseled tablets; they were created *by people*, and very specific people for specific purposes. But life all around us has changed, people and their needs have changed, and our structures and societal norms have shifted dramatically.

This moment has shown us that we can and should outgrow old ways. There is a mirror being held up to the sector and it must reckon with its own demons; this is the time to meet this moment of transformation. Unfortunately, those who dig their heads deeper in the sand and hang on tighter will be left behind. I've seen it firsthand with organizations that are waiting for their strategic plan to kick off, their fundraising drive to wrap up, their new hires to orient, or some elements of their weak organizational culture to be remedied, and as they wait for the "perfect time" to change, they continue to lose staff, revenue, and impact, until their disintegration reaches a crisis point. There is never a perfect time to shift your thinking and be better, but waiting until the breaking point is never the right time.

I hope you will meet this moment and overcome fear, dogmatism, the comfort of the status quo, and elevate, untether, and evolve your work into something different and better. One of my favorite quotes that now sits on my office wall is from Aaron Walker, founder and CEO of Camelback Ventures: "What we are fighting for has never existed."

What motivates my purpose and passion, and what I fight for, is the belief that we can create a world in which we all have access to prosperity, opportunity, and the choices to fully live in the freedom of our humanity. I share the dream of liberation with many colleagues in the sector, where power and oppression release their stranglehold on our individual and collective thoughts and behaviors. Our sector has taken baby steps toward change and it is not enough. Our ways of addressing social problems are often wasteful and ineffective. People just like you can use new skills and strategies that fit *this* time of growing uncertainty and possibility to create a new future for the sector and our world.

## Why We Must Pause for Change

My business name, Pause for Change, and the PAUSE acronym (as the framework) came to be because the most common advice I most frequently share with clients is to *slow down, pause, take a timeout*. Pausing is the first and most important step to creating change—pausing to identify that there is uncertainty, acknowledging that there is an opportunity to create deeper impact, and making the decision to take action in new ways.

In the social sector, we work quickly to meet the needs of our many stakeholders and we are rewarded for not pausing—for rushing to solutions, working too many hours for not enough pay, and exhausting our personal resources to aid others. Not only must we disrupt this expectation and celebrated behavior of overwork and overwhelm, but also we must ask ourselves, What good, long-lasting, powerful change has ever resulted from a rush job led by people who are beyond burnout?

While the work of social impact is tremendously busy and complex, the PAUSE framework is comprised of simple skills you can use anytime you experience uncertainty and want to save time and resources and create deeper change.

The five skills are:

**P:** Package the Challenge
**A:** Assess Uncertainty
**U:** Understand Stakeholders
**S:** Solution Testing
**E:** Evidence-Informed Decision-Making

The PAUSE skills help people and organizations address challenges and opportunities more effectively, whether they are looking at incremental improvement or trying to create disruptive change. I will use the word "challenge" to describe the focus of this work, and while some projects are truly about exploring a promising opportunity, there is still a challenge at the heart of that exploration, so I'll use "challenge" in the rest of the book to keep it simple.

Some of these skills make logical sense at face value, and others need a bit more explanation. As you work through this book, I'll give you many examples from real clients of what each of these letters and skills means and how the skills are applied "in real life." This book is divided into two sections, Part One: What's Dysfunctional about Status Quo Problem-Solving? and Part Two: How Do We Make Change Using the PAUSE Skills? I wanted to dedicate space to talk about what is messed up about how we work and why I think it is this way, and then dedicate the majority of the content to sharing what all of us can do differently.

It makes my heart sing that I get to share some of the stories I have accumulated from my own experiences and my work with clients. I am thrilled to share these examples beyond the four walls of a workshop because they are powerful, illustrative, and, I hope, inspiring. I want to acknowledge that these stories are my recollections of these events. I have done my best to mask the identities of the individuals without losing the essence of the tale, and although I use "I" for simplicity, these stories were at times experienced with my former cofounder Amelia and other coaches, with leaders and staff from organizations, and with stakeholders, all of whom still take up residence in my heart. Their trust in me and in the process has made all of my learning possible and has benefited the current and future clients whom I have the honor to support.

My hope is that as you read this book you will pause at each stage to apply the activities to your work or an actual challenge (as an individual or with a team). I'm not a fan of the theoretical, and most people learn by action, so I would love for you to complete the activities and document your learning (and in the future, integrate the PAUSE skills into your daily practice). To improve your self-awareness, please pause to consider the questions at the end of each chapter and reflect on the ways that you are transformed on this learning journey.

I want to be clear, as I am with people who hire me to support their organizations, that I am not like traditional consultants. I do not have the answers to how you should address your challenges. I know this because most likely I am not your stakeholder. What I *do* know is that I provide the skills and support that will empower you to know how best to get clarity and take action based on evidence.

If you use these skills, you will know if a problem really is a problem, what people need most, and, through rapid testing, which solution will actually work (or not) and why. I also want to acknowledge that I speak from what I have experienced and learned up to now, and I will continue to integrate new learning from all the delicious concepts, conversations, missteps (yes, they are part of it!), methodologies, writings, and big, bold questions to which I am continually exposed.

If you want to go deeper in your learning journey, please connect with me at heather@pauseforchange.com or learn more at PauseforChange.com. I'd love to learn about your organization and your challenges, and explore how I can help. Enjoy the book, and thanks for reading!

# Let's Talk about Positionality

BEFORE WE jump into discussing the dysfunction of our problem-solving methods in the social sector, I want to first talk about positionality. Positionality essentially means that *you* see the world as *you* see the world based on your past and current life and the numerous factors that have shaped who you are. Positionality, and recognizing the uniqueness of each of our perspectives, makes sense to consider, but it is an important factor we rarely pause to analyze.

It is imperative that we show up to this work after first acknowledging how we arrive, what our identities are, how they were and are shaped, and how they have been and are intertwined with the power we hold (or don't). I won't go into all of the various forms, types, and frameworks of power, but essentially, *you and I are designers, researchers, makers, creatives, leaders (whether we hold those titles or not). If we help create something from nothing, who we are gets infused into that work. When we hold the role of creator and decision-maker, we have power, and our decisions create small and large impacts.*

As a note, when I talk about leaders, I am talking in terms of institutional power and rank. I prefer Margaret Wheatley's definition: "*A leader is anyone willing to help*, anyone who sees something that needs to change and takes the first steps to influence that situation" (original emphasis). But although I like this definition of "leader" because it is more egalitarian and accessible, for the points in this book, I am using the definition typically adopted within organizational hierarchies: a leader is whoever has the most power. And when I talk about power, I appreciate and am deeply intrigued by the definition given by Greater Good Studio's cofounder and executive director, Sara Cantor: "The ability to change another person's reality."

I want to use the Positionality Wheel to give you a little background about how my positionality and identities shape what I bring to my work, the power I hold, and why I see the world in the ways that I do. Without hearing my positionalities, human nature would predict that you would typically fill the gaps in your knowledge about me with assumptions, stereotypes, and projections. We all do it, and we've actually gotten unhealthily and expediently "good" at filling in these gaps, especially as we move faster and live more distracted.

Dr. Lesley-Ann Noel, assistant professor at the College of Design at North Carolina State University and coeditor of *The Black Experience in Design*, first introduced me to the Positionality Wheel along with her awesome Designer's Critical Alphabet, both of which she created in 2019. The Positionality Wheel is a fantastic tool for personal exploration into identity, intersectionality, power, and relationships. The twelve layers of positionality are embedded in systems, structures, and social constructs, and there are inherent unspoken and spoken benefits and deficits attributed to these different positionalities. Unfortunately, our systems and constructs rarely hold space for the complexities of who we are, let alone how our identities intersect in concert and evolve with time and life experiences. We have to pause and consider how we arrive at this work, and explore with each other how our power and positionalities shape our individual and collective possibilities.

I hope that by reading through my positionalities and seeing the lenses I apply to my life and work, you will add dimension and curiosity to the red-headed, freckled-faced woman in the picture and the short bio you read on the book cover. After you read about my past and present, I want you to pause and complete your own Positionality Wheel. Self-awareness is key, and taking time to think about where you've been and where you are can help you better design where you're headed. You will see a section called Pause and Consider in this chapter and in the chapters to follow that will guide you to complete your own activities. I believe in learning by doing, so this book is not meant to just inform but also have you immediately practice what you have learned and apply it to your work and life.

## My Positionality

This is not meant to be a mini autobiography but a way for you to better understand how I see the world and how I am impacted by my positionalities. I think it would be very helpful if more "thought leaders" shared their positionalities to help us better understand their perspectives and deepen our empathetic connections to the humans behind the work.

I also want to share my positionalities because we rarely spend enough time getting to know each other. Dominant culture often values rushed greetings and introductions that become stale—"what's your name and what do you do"—but there is always so much more important background just under the surface.

### Race and Ethnicity

I am white and non-Hispanic (by frustratingly limiting census standards), but I like to think of myself as white, tad Costa Rican, Euro mix.

My mom's name is Rosita Alvarado, and my grandmother Clotilde (Clotildita or Dita for short) was born and raised in San Jose, Costa Rica. She fell in love with a red-headed botanist from Boston. I joke that my grandfather went for Costa Rica's amazingly beautiful flora and fauna but discovered the rare species of woman that was my grandmother. She was the best storyteller, and our favorite activity was sitting at her tiny kitchen table spending hours looking through all of her photo albums and art books (her kitchen table is now my office desk). She expanded my mind and curiosity, sharing with me our rich family history, beautiful art, and her experiences becoming an American housewife, mother, and socialite wife to a rising academic professor and dean. Her thick accent and unique version of "Spanglish" were present and beloved until the day she died, just six months shy of one hundred years old.

I say I'm a Euro mix because in my family we've also got Mayflower ties on both sides, and I know English, Scottish, and Danish bloodlines are present. Unfortunately, my dad's side of the family is much less known, and in my mind, way less dramatic and intriguing than my Central American roots, so I use the catchall "Euro mix."

When I think about race and ethnicity, I also think about my parents, of course. Being part Latina definitely shaped my mom's worldview, and as an elementary school teacher, she dedicated her career to primarily teaching English as a second language. She engaged in social justice activities such as using her evenings to help prepare her students' parents for their naturalization exams. Mom is the dreamer who instilled in me that anything is possible. Dad, Hugh Dale, was the pragmatic

Air Force senior master sergeant, meteorologist, and hurricane hunter who wanted a budget and plan for how we would complete every idea. He engaged my love of debate and forced me to understand and verbalize multiple sides of an issue. Growing up with the two of them shaped the way I reach for the seemingly impossible while having a plan for how to get there. My experience of being a little sister to Julie, who is six years older, taught me to closely watch the decisions of others, to learn and integrate useful lessons.

### Age

As I write, I am forty-five years old, and, ooh-wee, what a journey of exquisite joy and sorrow it has been!

### Gender/Sexuality

I identify as a cisgender heterosexual woman, and I use the pronouns she/her/hers.

### Ability/Disability

I have an invisible disability: I am nearly deaf in my right ear. When I was just a little first-grade cutie, I was in a roller-skating accident that resulted in multiple skull fractures. After two surgeries, I was left with a slightly crooked smile due to facial paralysis, and a challenging road ahead. From the time I was eight, I sat at the right front of every classroom to favor my "good" ear. I learned to read lips, and I got my first hearing aid at nineteen. I have to worry about physical settings and how I will accommodate my own needs. I experience brain strain and fatigue caused by listening as hard as I can (yes, even with a hearing aid; they are not magic), and there are many times when I feel embarrassed, frustrated, left out, and sad when I am unable to fully engage.

## Marital Status

I'm a happily divorced co-parent who has spent eight years and counting with the most amazing partner.

## Parental Status

I am the mother of two teenagers. Parenting is hard, and I am forever balancing the thrill and inspiration of watching them grow, with utter exhaustion and the commitment required to be present and nurture them on their journey, especially while being a multipassionate entrepreneur.

## Where I Grew Up

We were restationed from Offutt Air Force Base in Nebraska to Phoenix, Arizona, when I was just three months old, so I consider myself a native Arizonan. I grew up in Maryvale, Arizona, which is a suburb in West Phoenix. What's interesting about where I grew up is that it's where I experienced being an "other" for the first time. Most of my community was Latine and I was surrounded by a diversity of food, language, and households. Of course, what I recall most was the fun I had playing games and riding bikes, but as an adult, I have learned so much more about the history and transformation of the Maryvale community, such as the reasons behind Maryvale's demographic shift from white to Latine: white flight, the destruction of six thousand homes for airport expansion, and environmental racism that still permeates the area (Maryvale was declared a superfund site due to TCE exposure in 1987).

My dad benefited from the GI Bill (a privilege my white father enjoyed but that excluded 1.2 million Black veterans) and got his degree in computer engineering. He retired after twenty-five years of Air Force service, and before I started third grade, we moved to a new part of central Phoenix so he could take a job as a software engineer.

The new neighborhood was all white and I experienced extreme culture shock. I didn't understand why my new friends had so much. I didn't understand why their houses were so big, why their moms didn't work, why they had so many Barbies and Cabbage Patch Kids, how they always went on vacation and ate out at restaurants. This is where I first saw the difference in wealth and privilege. This is also the first time I experienced being judged by another child or their parents as "less than."

I also grew up traveling primarily on public transportation. My mom has epilepsy, so she is unable to drive. We took buses to every appointment and errand when the car my dad drove was occupied. I know how one simple errand can take half a day and lots of planning, especially with two kids.

At the age of fifteen, I also grew up in an additional family. This is when I met my high school sweetheart, whom I later married and who became the father of my two children. His family was essentially the opposite of mine, and for more than a decade, until we cut all ties to his family, I experienced and watched, directly and indirectly, the impact of physical violence, drug abuse, incarceration, police violence, teen pregnancy, drive-by shootings, rape, severe mental illness, domestic violence, school dropout, drug dealing, homelessness, robbery, and sexual abuse. I used to meet others in my undergrad sociology classes who saw a list like this as a litany of theoretical "social challenges," but for years these "social ills" had faces and names, and were people I deeply cared for.

While I carry trauma connected to these experiences and I see the ripple of trauma in my own children, who never even met my ex-in-laws, I also feel privileged to have been shaped by these experiences. I saw the amount of energy it requires to choose a different path and the consequences you pay for it. I saw well-meaning social service professionals showing up with a microscopic band-aid to heal generations of chaos and trauma. I also saw the power of mentorship and how the support of just a few people can transform generations to come.

At the time of this writing, I live in sun-drenched Tucson, Arizona, and I believe we each have the responsibility to acknowledge the historical contexts in which we exist. I acknowledge that I conduct my work from the traditional and stolen homelands of the Tohono O'odham and Yaqui people and within a state that is comprised of twenty-two federally recognized tribes. These lands continue to carry their stories and struggles for survival and identity, and it is my responsibility and obligation to reflect on and actively address these histories. I want to honor their ancestors and their descendants today, including elders of the past, present, and future. Land acknowledgments are just one small part of disrupting and dismantling colonial structures. (This land acknowledgment has been adapted from and inspired by Monique Rivera and Rachael Dietkus.)

### Class or Status (as a Child and Today)

I would consider my family to have been middle class as I was growing up. Now, I would guess that I am upper-middle class because I have access to resources that I can invest in retirement and I have adequate savings with little debt (a privileged benefit of my position in the widening racial wealth gap).

### Level of Education

I have a bachelor's degree in sociology with a focus on social injustice and a minor in African American studies, later called Africana studies. I have a master's degree in public health with a focus on health disparities. People often think it's interesting that I was a white red-headed girl in this area of study (and only one of a few white folks in my Africana studies courses, and the only white volunteer and later employee for three years at my university's African American Cultural Resource Center), but I was comfortable in the discomfort and it helped shape who I am today.

## What I Do for a Living

I became a consultant because I was disenchanted with working in the social sector and I was motivated to change it. In my career, I have followed a very winding path, which I highly encourage. After my master's, I worked in university campus health as a health educator; oversaw NIH-funded research studies in hospital emergency departments; worked on national initiatives to grow translational bench-to-bedside research; and in nonprofits, designed curriculum, interventions, and programs, wrote grants, and fundraised. Later, I coached lean innovation in for-profit companies and then pivoted to dedicate the last many years to working with nonprofits, philanthropic foundations, and local governments to create what is now the PAUSE framework.

I've had the honor of working with both tiny and very large organizations, including more than a dozen organizations in a small, rural, desert community of fewer than three thousand people, and with one of the largest and most well-known US nonprofits. While I've worked with global organizations and national funders, I've also had the privilege of working in local communities with city governments, foundations, and nonprofits.

## Languages I Speak and Why

I speak English and can understand a lot more Spanish than I can speak, but if I spend more than a few days in a Spanish-speaking country, it comes back.

I would like to add the caveat that I have lived exclusively in the United States (even though I've had the great privilege to travel internationally), and all of my work to date has been serving US-based social impact organizations. While I mostly present a US-based perspective, I feel confident that the PAUSE framework is transferable to other countries, with the assumption that some additional adaptation might be required based on diverse cultural norms and practices.

Now that you have read my twelve aspects of positionality (and I went into much more detail than what you typically reflect on a Positionality Wheel), I hope you can see the value of going deeper rather than seeing me as just Heather Hiscox, founder and CEO of Pause for Change. You learned what you might never have expected by looking at me, such as challenges that shaped my life, and how I come to do this work. These twelve elements of my positionality also come with more or less power, some that I am automatically assigned and I have not earned. I try to pay attention to interactions and relationships in which I hold power, especially when I work with clients and community stakeholders. I also actively seek to share and give away my power to people and groups who have been excluded from decision-making roles. Any consideration of positionality should be paired with considerations of power.

Can you imagine how your level of connection, understanding, and empathy would shift if you took the time to not only think through your own journey as framed by these positionalities and how they impact your work, but also understand the positionalities from which your colleagues were working? What if you understood the positionalities of the stakeholders you support?

## PAUSE AND CONSIDER

**YOU WILL** see these Pause and Consider sections through-out the book. I assume that your professional and personal lives are fast-paced, and I know that it can be hard to build in time for reflection, but it is so essential for growth and change. I hope these provocations help you not only pro-cess the content and make progress on your own specific challenge but also stimulate new thinking and conversation inside your organization.

While this tool can be very powerful to complete and share in team settings, for now, I want you to use the Posi-tionality Wheel for the purpose of personal introspection. You may be thinking, "Hold on a minute. I just want simple skills to improve my work!" I hear you, but one major insight I learned very early on is that people who have trouble inte-grating the PAUSE framework often lack self-awareness. Many of these individuals do not notice how their impatience, tendency to talk over others, never making time for connec-tion, and frequent misalignment between their words and actions impact their ability to learn and, many times, how they are perceived by others. These behaviors can be toxic both personally and within an organizational culture. The good news is that if you see these traits in yourself, your col-leagues, or your leaders, they can be addressed, *with effort*.

Imagine now that you are writing the introduction to your own book and sharing your positionalities. How would you answer the prompts below, and what insights come up for you? You don't have to fact-check, share with others, or be validated for what you write here. You just have to think them through and, if you like, document your answers.

Please also consider how your positionalities are connected to power, and how your power has an impact. Walking through these twelve areas of positionality will help improve your self-awareness and ground you for your future work. Even though it is not a specific, separate skill in the framework, pausing to reflect and integrate insights is the thread that binds each skill.

Race and ethnicity
Age
Gender/sexuality
Ability/disability
Marital status
Parental status
Where you grew up
Class or status (as a child)
Class or status (today)
Level of education
What you do for a living
Languages you speak and why

Now that you have completed the activity, please consider the following prompts to see what insights bubble up for you.

- How did that feel?

- What stood out to you the most? Any "aha" moments, or insights?

- How do you think your positionalities and life experiences shape how you see the world?

- Where do you feel visible and invisible?

- What assumptions have you made about others when you have not understood their positionalities? Do you think assumptions have ever been made about you?

- Are there ways that you might integrate positionalities in how you think about or conduct your work (or even show up socially, personally)?

- Which of your positionalities are connected to power? How are they connected to power? How does this power show up in your work, on purpose or unintentionally?

# The Tension between Loving and Hating the Sector

DON'T REALLY like saying that I hate the sector, since "hate" is such a strong word (and I truly lean toward hope, faith, and possibility), but I feel like it needs to be said that we can both appreciate and want to tear apart the sector at the same time. That is tension I think we all hold to some extent as social sector change agents. It is essential and constructive that we talk about what is not working and what can be reimagined.

For me, the core of the tension is that we exist to help, but at times we harm and defeat. While we feed, clothe, and shelter people, we also dehumanize people. We want people and communities to win, but often our paperwork, policies, politics, processes, and power win. We are many times complacent with our status quo beliefs and behaviors, even when we know there is a problem or something doesn't make sense. We sometimes exert our power and privilege to do nothing about it.

My social sector career has been filled with highs and lows—I have experienced the best *and* worst of who we are. Each project, boss, board, and mission has shaped me and the PAUSE framework. My positionality and these experiences have shaped my identity and what I care about, just as they do for you.

I want to go deeper to unpack why I feel love *and* hate. I love the sector because I believe in what is possible for social change, because most of my friends and colleagues are in some way connected to social impact work, and because I have directly benefited from its programs and resources. In the year between undergrad and grad school, I decided to move from a student role to a staff position for a program I loved. I transitioned from being a college coach at two rural high schools focused on helping ethnically diverse, first-generation, and low-income students get the skills and assistance they needed to be college-ready, to spending one year redesigning all of the program curricula for more than forty school sites. I was paid a pittance and given no benefits. During that year, I got very sick and had no health coverage. It was a lovely doctor at a federally qualified health care center who diagnosed and treated my concurrent ear, sinus, and lung infections and charged me only $25 to get the antibiotics I needed to heal after weeks of pain. When my dad was sick for about a decade before he passed, it was a nonprofit CEO who walked me through what I needed to know about caregiving and end-of-life planning. When I was first introduced to social entrepreneurship, I leaned on local small business programming made possible by local and national funders. When I needed resources to help me navigate domestic abuse, I had amazing and 100 percent free support to name and process my trauma.

There was also support I should have taken but didn't out of shame. After my divorce, I hit a real low financially, and at that time one of my very first clients was a food bank. My task was to help them codesign a new program to provide rainwater harvesting for households that are often excluded from access to sustainability resources. No one, personally or professionally, had any idea that I had only $50 left in my checking account. I was trying to figure out how to buy groceries for the week, and those food boxes looked really good. I was too ashamed to ask for one because I did not want to impact my client relationship or their perception of my ability to provide quality consulting. There is also aid that I have not yet accessed but just knowing it's there makes me feel supported. My daughter is queer (shared with full permission from my amazing girl), and I am so thankful that we have not only friends and family to help her on her journey but also some really lovely LGBTQ2+-supporting organizations that we can go to for extra resources and connection.

I've also experienced being revictimized by legal advocates ignorant of domestic abuse dynamics. I still navigate awful options for self-paid, self-employed health care coverage, and witness the lack of and result of weak start-up ecosystems that exclude the most underestimated and under-resourced people in our communities. It is no shocker that I care deeply about the causes of food justice, domestic abuse, LGBTQ2+ rights, entrepreneurship, and equitable and affordable health care access. These issues are deeply personal for me, and many of us do work that is deeply personal. In other words, for many of us in the sector, these social issues are not about idealistic, lofty aspirations for care and justice; they impact us and the people we love every day.

We all bring not only the issues we care about with us to work but our past professional experiences as well. It can be helpful to acknowledge both the highs *and* lows of our social impact work. Before I even started exploring what has become the PAUSE framework, my winding journey included some extraordinary professional wins and losses. For three years, every two weeks I volunteered and codesigned educational sessions all about diverse health topics, with a group of mostly older Spanish-speaking Latinas called Las Nanas. They nourished me in so many ways, quite literally (and deliciously!), and showed me the power of community elders and codesign. On another leg of my journey, I helped execute part of the crowdfunding campaign that launched the first-ever academic journal focused solely on transgender issues, called *Transgender Studies Quarterly*. Later I was able to coach the chief fundraiser at Trans Lifeline, a suicide prevention hotline for transgender people. In another role, I helped train a beautifully scrappy, grassroots-led organization on how to have a capital campaign that helped them buy a new space before theirs was bulldozed for urban expansion.

Other times, I made some serious errors. I designed curricula for stakeholders and never once consulted them. I tried to launch the first satellite office of a social impact accelerator and forgot to talk about money and legal first, ultimately disintegrating the opportunity. As a newbie to the social impact codesign space, I repeatedly fell into competitive traps that killed collaborations, and I stayed quiet when I saw unethical behavior at more than three of my nonprofit employers. These flaws and failures are hard to admit, but they were also tremendous learning opportunities that shifted my values, how I choose whom I work with, and how I show up to this work. We all have (and often hide) shameful missteps, but this is a time of reckoning for not only the sector but also us individuals to consider how we can be better and position ourselves for creating deeper impact in our organizations and communities.

I must also address the fact that many of us have suffered organizational trauma, and this trauma has physical, emotional, cognitive, and behavioral implications. In a

Trauma-Responsive Design class by Rachael Dietkus, MSW, LCSW, founder of Social Workers Who Design, I learned certain terms connected with organizational trauma. They include "moral injury," "institutional injury/betrayal," "institutional failure," and "shadow values." Moral injury is the feeling you get when you perform or see behaviors that go against your personal values and moral beliefs. Institutional injury/betrayal and institutional failure result when organizations create negative or entirely ineffective actions on which individuals, internal or external, are dependent. Shadow values in many ways connect these types of trauma—the shadow refers to the negative, often unstated "real values" of an organization's culture that lie secretly behind the organization's outward or publicly stated values. The chasm between what is and what something is meant or expected to be can create significant cognitive dissonance and distrust, and can be very traumatizing. When I learned these terms, I found them hugely validating; these realities, while very real and damaging, are often denied and suppressed by the organizations causing the harm, which compounds the exhaustion and compassion fatigue that we already experience and that impact how we learn and show up to address challenges.

A few years back, I presented at The Network for Social Work Management's annual conference. In another talk, one of the other presenters mentioned something called attention deficit traits, or ADT. They reported that signs of ADT are being seen in a growing number of workplaces (and this was even before COVID-19). The signs include doing "more with less," taxing work conditions, distractibility, inner frenzy, impatience, and inability to process, prioritize, and respond effectively. Working in harmful and chaotic settings and cultures will absolutely impact how we feel while we work and how we treat our colleagues and stakeholders.

## Our Desire to Help Can Create Harm

One of my favorite parts about the social sector is our commitment and desire to help, but this is also one of our deepest flaws. I have had the privilege of working with some of the most committed and passionate sector professionals across nonprofits, local governments, and philanthropic foundations, whose careers and identities are connected to their need to serve. Unfortunately, this desire to help can create significant gaps in understanding and is one of the most highly problematic aspects of how we address challenges.

The ways we help are often tied to the notions of providing services *to* our stakeholders or creating programs *for* our stakeholders. Language is very important, and the use of "to" and "for" create separation and the dichotomies of "us and them," provider and recipient, benefactor and beneficiary, and program designer/deliverer and program consumer/user. This language not only devalues our stakeholders as passive recipients but also places power in the hands of those who provide support. The words we use to talk about community members are rife with power dynamics. Some like to use the words "clients," "recipients," "beneficiaries," "constituents," "partners," or "customers." I wish there was a perfect word that reflected less of a focus on service and emphasized authentic relationships, respect, and shared power. For the purpose of this book, I will mainly use "stakeholders" and "community members that we support."

This "us and them" mentality in our white-dominated sector often shows up as white saviorism, the savior complex, and what Dr. Ibram X. Kendi calls "Savior Theology." Dr. Kendi discusses how this idea of "I'm here to save you!" is actually one of the oldest racist ideas. These false narratives of "saving" and "helping," refined and sustained for almost six hundred years, are dangerous and threaten how we show up for our communities and colleagues.

This saviorist motivation may be unexpressed, but it usually pops up in our problem-solving arrogance of "I/we know what *you/they* need." Instead of integrating elements of codesign and creating "with" and "by" our stakeholders, we base our work on assumptions that do not provide space for learning from the lived *and living* experiences of our stakeholders. I use the terms "lived" and "living experience" (a riff on the term "living experts" used by Creative Reaction Lab) together, rather than using just "lived experience," as the people we learn from and with are experiencing joy and struggle each and every day. These are not past realities but ever-present. I also want to call out that there are various definitions of "codesign"—what it means, who "really" does it, what is nonnegotiable, and what's not enough. Our definitions and conversations about codesign are essential to the evolution of this work, and I am fortunate to have amazing colleagues whom I can turn to for advice, dissent, and support.

Just as our language and white saviorism can create harmful separation, by not seeing each other's positionalities and power, we also miss out on seeing each other's abundance. I love the model of community cultural wealth by Dr. Tara Yosso, which I feel captures so many assets that we often overlook when designing programs and strategies and was introduced to me by Michael O'Bryan, founder of design strategy firm Humanature. Dr. Yosso outlines six forms of cultural capital: aspirational, familial, social, navigational, resistant, and linguistic. I won't go into detail for each of the six forms of capital, but in summary, they include the ability to stay hopeful while navigating persistent barriers, the development of skills for opposing inequality, the powerful benefits of multilingual and multicultural fluency, an expanded sense of familial and community connection that is larger than one's self, and the savvy of navigating social institutions and leveraging the power of peer and social connections for support.

Can you imagine what it would look like if we as a sector switched from seeing our stakeholders as passive recipients to seeing them as abundant with capital, strengths, assets, experiences, talents, and abilities? If we recognized these forms of capital, it would be ridiculously closed-minded *not* to tap into this power and potential to create greater impact.

This also speaks to the importance of diversity within organizations and teams. *The more homogenous your talent and teams, the more limited your viewpoints and possibilities.* One of the greatest ways the sector can improve its outcomes is to improve its inclusion and treatment of internal and external stakeholders. This is where power and positionality absolutely must be recognized, because for an inexcusably long time, leaders in the sector have opted out of focusing on diversity, equity, inclusion, and belonging inside and outside their organizations, and this has created tremendous harm in a sector that purports to help.

I have been both saddened and encouraged when I hear from colleagues of color that for the first time, they are seeing their own presence as staff in the social sector as a powerful contribution. Many of these colleagues have been treated like their position is a gift; they are ignored, superficially engaged, and often tokenized, asked to represent an entire group of people that includes tremendous intradiversity. They are also often misjudged and mischaracterized. More than one colleague has shared how their sector colleagues have assumed that because they are non-white, they represent a stereotype or false narrative, including that they grew up "on the mean streets," had single mothers, struggled with education, or grew up in poverty. One colleague shared that they had to laugh when this happened, as both of their parents are Ivy League university professors!

No one deserves to be treated as suspect or less than or relegated to "beneficiary-only" status. The diversity of the experiences of all of our stakeholders, inside and outside of our organizations, is the ultimate untapped and unappreciated asset and can be the foundation for our future impact. All of our individual and collective experiences and identities can be the fuel for our work in social change.

## Our Status Quo Problem-Solving Skills Are Outdated and Insufficient

As I've shared, I was motivated to develop this framework mainly because as a sector we do not have efficient and effective ways to address challenges. What problem-solving looks like currently relies most often on

- good intentions,
- building what you think should work,
- designing solutions in a bubble or in silos,
- copying "best practices,"
- waiting six months or a year to see results, and
- investing in pilot studies/programs.

In fact, most organizations do not have a problem-solving policy or methodology. What organizations usually do have are *unspoken and uninterrogated habits* for how they address challenges. While it might feel normal to activate the usual habits that your organization supports (and be rewarded for replicating those habits), it's unfortunately also normal to not consider your habits at all. Studies show that about half of our behaviors are dictated by our habits, so we are on autopilot about half the time, and when habits are unrecognized, they can be hard to change.

A habit loop begins with a cue. A cue is something in the environment out of our control that kicks off some sort of action. The action is what we can control, and once an action is taken to address the cue, there is a resulting or desired reward. The rewards that we most often crave include certainty, progress, impact, and benefit. How we get there most effectively and efficiently is dictated by the actions we take.

Here are just some standard cues in social impact:

- Evaluating whether it makes sense to implement a request from an internal leader, board member, or funder

- Addressing a drop in recruitment and/or retention of internal or external stakeholders

- Identifying whether a "best practice" from another organization will address a challenge in your organization

- Figuring out the best way to achieve a goal outlined in your strategic plan

- Accelerating outcomes on initiatives that have stalled or lack progress

- Uncovering how to address a concern raised by the public

- Addressing unpredictable demographic, economic, financial, and political shifts that are impacting the communities and organizations you support

- Figuring out how to prioritize and align your work with resources

- Supporting the exploration of bold new ideas that, while potentially impactful, come with risk and unknown return on investment (ROI)

- Addressing internal organizational issues like culture, communication, and teamwork

While unacknowledged habits can be dangerous, so are cues (e.g., the issues, problems, opportunities you want to address). Cues often create the feeling of uncertainty, and the human body *despises* uncertainty. Uncertainty creates a threat response in our bodies that our brain perceives as pain. Uncertainty can make us feel powerless and confused. It causes headaches, back tension, stomachaches, and panic. Addressing uncertainty also makes our brains work harder and we have to use more energy, of which our bodies are also not a fan.

When we feel uncertain and therefore uncomfortable, we want to come up with the antidote as quickly as possible to try to extinguish our discomfort. Guess what? Decision-making, planning, and all the activities that give us what I call the "illusion of certainty" are here to save the day! When we choose a path forward, our body rewards us with a flood of new chemicals that make us feel so much better. Full of dopamine, we now feel in control, we can relax, and we can move forward from our sticking points.

Understanding the biology behind our actions is important; it explains why we as individuals—and the sector as a whole—choose to stick with what we are used to and avoid uncertainty. Unfortunately, while our status quo problem-solving habits make biological sense, these habits can waste resources, cause harm, and increasingly make little sense in today's world. At times we would rather stick with what's known (even when we know it's ineffective) rather than try something new that might open up amazing possibilities (and also invite additional uncertainty). This reluctance to explore new strategies is highly problematic in the social sector because it limits our ability to address our major and growing social challenges in new ways.

I shared a call with an individual who has been working in the area of affordable housing for more than twenty-five years. (To protect people's identities, I will use pseudonyms here and in other stories.) Victor told me that he'd had a video chat with colleagues with whom he's worked for those two and half decades, and he said to them, "I think we need to really rethink our work. It's obvious that what we've been doing is not working and things are worse than they've ever been. What are we doing wrong? What could we be doing differently?" When he told me what he had asked, not only did I love his bold and rarely asked questions, but I was excited to hear the answers from his colleagues about how they might retool and remobilize their efforts. Unfortunately, this was not the response he received. Instead, Victor said, "They looked at me like I was a weirdo, and asked me, 'What are you talking about?'"

Can you imagine how he must have felt? Here he was, asking very important, albeit difficult questions, driven by passion to create greater impact and he was shut down. As a result of their responses, he is now doubling down on his efforts to break down silos, forming new cross-sector and cross-community alliances, and looking for new strategies to integrate into his work, leaving his colleagues stuck in the status quo, behind.

When I worked in organizations, we rarely paused to ask big questions about our impact, and like Victor, I was often shut down when I did ask them. We rarely asked, "Are we really moving the needle?" We just kept working, having meetings, and producing predictable outcomes. I always felt like such a troublemaker because I was always asking questions like, "Is this the right thing to do? Does what we are doing connect with our mission? Do we really want to align with that donor or that partner?" I often got the "weirdo look" and was asked, "What are you talking about?" So often, when "troublemakers" ask these larger questions, we move them to the margins.

When we move people to the margins, they are often labeled as "radical." If you were to look up the word—as I did because I enjoy doing it as a grounding practice—you'd find that it has several meanings, among them getting to the root or origin of something, favoring reform, and challenging what is accepted and traditional. Although the intent in labeling someone or something as radical is often exclusion and degradation, to be called radical is what we all should aspire to because it means we are holding ourselves accountable and ensuring that we are actually helping create healthy and equitable futures for all.

I feel like this is our "time's up" moment in the sector. We can't keep working in the same ways if we want to make greater systemic and sustainable change. COVID-19 has shown us very clearly areas where we are deeply flawed and how we will continue to face increasing uncertainty. There has never been a better time to pause, listen, and explore the rich and important answers to the questions we rarely ask. When these big, bold questions are asked, they should not further divide the sector or our organizations into two camps of "complacent" versus "troublemaking," but should move us all toward greater accountability and impact.

The bold questions we need to ask include:

- What's working? What's not?

- What happens when we keep doing what we've always done?

- What could be possible if we shifted the habits of how we work?

- What are the habits we have established as an organization that make shifting and working in new ways harder and continually delayed?

- What are the cues, problems, and challenges we need to address?

- What actions do we typically take?

- How are we rewarding action?

- How might we be pushing new ideas and people to the margins?

We know that we have new challenges and others that have not yet emerged. We can't keep using skills that were designed in the past to fit challenges of the past. We need new skills that are flexible and ever-evolving to match our murky futures. The PAUSE skills are about shifting how we work and providing a framework that acknowledges our biology, organizational cultures, and larger systems.

## PAUSE AND CONSIDER

**YOU ARE** not alone if you've ever felt dissatisfied with the ways that you work, the organizational culture you function within, and the outcomes you create, intended and unintended. I used to be right there with you, struggling to understand how I could thrive in a sector that felt so fulfilling *and* so flawed. You have the power to shift your work, and it begins with pausing to notice those sources of tension, incongruencies, and opportunities for change. Consider these questions:

- What do you love about the sector? What do you (gulp) hate about the sector?

- What are the highs and lows you experience or have experienced in the sector? Can you identify organizational trauma you have experienced? Or even that you might have unintentionally caused?

- Think of wins and missteps you have experienced. What lessons did you learn from your successes and "failures"?

- Are there ways that you or your organization has fallen into the trap of creating *for* or providing services *to* stakeholders, rather than codesigning *with* and *by* stakeholders? Why do you think this is or was your approach?

- How do you and your organization perceive, recognize, and include the assets, abilities, and abundance of your internal and external stakeholders? Consider your colleagues, partners, and community members.

- What problem-solving habits do you or your organization currently practice?

- Are there cues that seem to push you and your organization to take action? What actions do you or your organization most often take?

- How are you currently rewarded for navigating uncertainty or taking action when you do see a problem or opportunity?

# 3

# Our Desire to Take Action Creates Waste at Scale

RELATED TO our status quo problem-solving habits and our love of action as an antidote to uncertainty, when we see a problem, we are rewarded for moving forward, making a plan, and getting results. There are some who believe that ideas themselves are useless and that execution is everything. Not only is this totally expressive of the white dominant culture's focus on "one right way," either/or, and urgency thinking, but it also creates a scenario in which we are judged by what we create and what we complete, and we are not supported for what we learn, for understanding the "why" behind our actions, and for how we make evidence-informed decisions.

While we all might feel less physical and emotional distress when we choose a path forward, we also can create a ton of unintentional waste. When I talk about "waste" I mean wasted time, money, energy, room in the mission—really, every activity that goes into making something possible, normally referred to as the "blood, sweat, and tears" behind any outcome.

By taking action, we often lull ourselves into believing that we are creating impact with the act of creating a plan itself, while in fact, we usually do not have the information we need to make fully informed decisions. In other words, *we conflate execution with impact.* We are really good at creating visual and written expressions of how things should work, usually in the forms of our grant proposals, logic models, Gantt charts, and program designs. We like to represent our work like it's clean, under control, and spot-on.

These types of plans might be normal and expected in the sector, and even very soothing, but in your experience, when has any one of those plans gone 100 percent as designed? We humans and our plans rarely account for the unknown and unexpected. The challenges we exist to address are very complex, and we have a hard time not only embracing that complexity but also providing mechanisms, allowances, structures, communication, and rewards that recognize and account for it. With the new lenses this work has given me, where some people see a plan's order and structure, I often see illusions of certainty and a written collection of untested assumptions.

I refer to this image as the "giant triangle of waste" and this is how most people and organizations work in the sector. Moving from bottom to top, the status quo problem-solving process often is built upon an unstable foundation and grows more fragile as the work and resources increase. The process usually begins with noticing that there is an issue—in other words, that something is not working or that something new might be possible. There is usually some symptom that indicates an opportunity for exploration. This stage is accompanied by

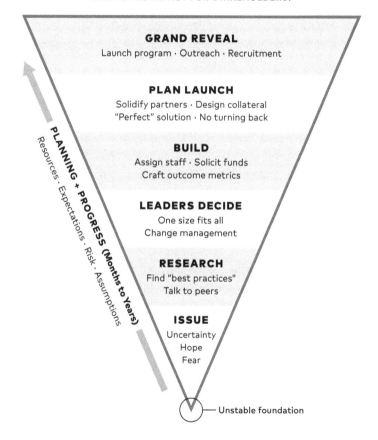

WHAT'S THE IMPACT FOR STAKEHOLDERS?

**GRAND REVEAL**
Launch program · Outreach · Recruitment

**PLAN LAUNCH**
Solidify partners · Design collateral
"Perfect" solution · No turning back

**BUILD**
Assign staff · Solicit funds
Craft outcome metrics

**LEADERS DECIDE**
One size fits all
Change management

**RESEARCH**
Find "best practices"
Talk to peers

**ISSUE**
Uncertainty
Hope
Fear

PLANNING + PROGRESS (Months to Years)
Resources · Expectations · Risk · Assumptions

Unstable foundation

feelings of hope for change, but often a lot of fear and uncertainty as well.

The next step usually takes the form of research into the problem as a way to take initial action and assuage discomfort. Research might include exploring what other people and organizations have done to tackle the same or similar issue, and investigating "best practices," which are usually the most eye-catching and feel most promising. Finding this information is usually assigned to a staff member to later be presented to a leader or decision-maker.

Next is the time when leaders usually step in and select a path forward. Leaders will often analyze the research, seek out additional information, and then filter what they've gathered through their own lenses of positionality and experiences. It is super common that one solution is selected and expected to work for all stakeholders. The decision at this point could be challenged, but most often, leaders initiate "change management" strategies to inform staff of what solution has been chosen and how they will play their roles in bringing the solution to life.

This next phase now moves the potential solution toward becoming reality. Staff are told who will do what and by when, expectations and outcomes are solidified, and if funding is required, funds will be sought by describing the dream outcome and how the organization will make it happen. As staff create and make decisions, dopamine continues to flood their brains, and they feel more connected as they see their ideas manifest in the forms of plans, models, handouts, curriculum, websites, and so on.

As the work progresses, fine-tuning occurs and the solution solidifies. Partnerships might be finalized, the design or more specific elements of the solution are completed, and the launch is steadily approaching. The solution often feels more "high stakes" at this point because staff are accountable for reaching their goals and people, internally and externally, are watching. The organization needs to deliver.

So "the moment" of launch or implementation arrives. This is when the solution that staff have been tirelessly constructing behind the scenes is unveiled and shared with stakeholders. For external-facing launches, it usually looks like some sort of grand reveal, where a solution is made as "perfect" as possible and then the stakeholder is "let in" to join the program and use a service. For internal-facing launches, this same "giant triangle" usually culminates in a new policy or work process that is once again "revealed," and then staff are expected to fall into step.

Key to this increasingly widening and unstable triangle is the final image of the stakeholders, placed outside of the process, waiting to experience the impact. So, what impact will your potential solution create? How does your solution best address the stakeholder's problem? How does the stakeholder access and experience impact from your solution?

As the amount of planning and progress increases, the organization becomes more and more committed—they allocate time, money, and energy, and also significant risk, assumptions, and expectations, often over months or years. Can't you just imagine the program coordinators, directors, and frontline staff sitting in extensive meetings? Can you envision the whiteboard drawings? Can you see the third cup of coffee sitting on the grant writer's secondhand desk as they pour over a logic model for a potential grant application to scrape together $3,500? Okay, I went too deep, but the point is that the "giant triangle" uses up a ton of energy, passion, purpose, hours/days/months, space in the mission, potential power, potential impact, and so on. Now imagine that these same scenarios and triangles of waste are being created in nearly every social impact organization, in every community. Think of the potential waste we are creating as we try to address some of the world's most important problems!

The other bad news is that our plans rarely go the way they're intended. In my years working on a huge variety of projects in a wide array of organizations, more than half of the projects that clients have in mind or think they are hiring me to help them build never see the light of day. Why? Because the proposed solutions are usually built on unstable foundations, and most have never touched the real lives of stakeholders, be it a frontline staff member, an agency partner, or a person in the community.

## Why Solutions Fail

The most common reasons a solution does not work fall into a few main (but definitely not exclusive) categories:

- The stakeholder does not want the solution.

- The stakeholder has another solution in mind that will better address their challenge.

- The stakeholder has another problem you were not aware of, or that you did not consider, that is a higher priority.

These categories make logical sense, but emotionally they can feel devastating. Here you have an organization's leadership and staff who have poured extensive time and energy into a potential solution, and with great pride, they offer it to stakeholders. They wait for the reward of a job well done and lives transformed because of the work they did.

But what if stakeholders reject the solution? What if stakeholders don't sign up, don't attend, don't comply, or don't complete? Ugh, it can feel like a gut punch, frustrating, defeating, and mystifying. When this happens, some organizations have a reflexive response, and it often manifests as a mental yelling at the stakeholder: "Hey! We made this for you!" Staff who designed the solution worked hard! They thought it all through, they had a plan, they followed orders, they told people about the solution, so why isn't it working?! Why aren't *they* (the stakeholders) using it?! Many organizations will continue to ram the proverbial square peg into the round hole, doing things like shifting logistics such as time and place, increasing outreach (new and more messaging), or conducting additional training, all with increasing frustration.

There are a few beliefs that motivate this continued pushing. The first belief is that "if *they* only knew about X, they would take part in Y/do Y/use Y." This pushing is reinforced by one of the most prevalent and harmful beliefs in the sector— that you are losing traction or not meeting your goals because "you are a best-kept secret." I wish more organizations would stop thinking they need to improve marketing and outreach and pause to consider how their programs miss the mark or lack value.

I want to note that I will use variations of the terms "value" and "create value," and I acknowledge that "value" is a term most often used in the for-profit business world, usually connected to creating useful products and services. While I don't want to get into the "is social impact also a business?" debate, I want to say that I intentionally adopt and use this term because far too often in social impact we lose sight of the fact that our jobs are to address social issues by creating value for our stakeholders. While the capitalistic, for-profit-related reference might make some uncomfortable, I am using the term to reinforce what I view as the purpose of our work as changemakers.

Another prevalent belief is that stakeholders will or must engage in every intervention. This especially holds true the more the stakeholders are perceived to have needs. This is problematic in ways that I will address further in later chapters, but what is at play is that instead of organizations looking inward to analyze what assumptions they missed and how they unintentionally created massive waste, they blame stakeholders for not engaging in the solution. This is one of the key manifestations of paternalism and white saviorism, and it turns the dynamic from "Hey! I made this for you!" into "Hey! What is wrong with you that you don't want this?!"

This sounds so nasty and harsh—the idea of being angry at those you exist to support! Sadly, I have seen it time and time again. Most significant and upsetting is that it reveals not only the disconnect with our shared humanity and the unrecognized empathy deficit that plagues the sector, but also the degree to which we have bought into status quo problem-solving, the "giant triangle" approach, and the belief in our own infallibility.

When you pause, step back, and work to understand *why* someone may not want to engage in an intervention, it usually makes perfect sense. Let me share one of my favorite examples.

A colleague of mine—I'll call him Joseph—was in a meeting with community members who were enrolled in a program he led, and in that meeting, there happened to also be a long-time CEO from a partner agency. Susan was seen as one of the top nonprofit CEOs and for many decades had run some of the community's largest organizations. She asked one of the community members present, Donna, why she believed people were not taking advantage of the home visit–based program that her agency was offering. Donna was kind enough to offer her hypothesis. The first question she asked Susan was,

"Do your staff go to people's homes in a car with the agency's logo on it?" Susan answered yes, and Donna then shared that even if the program was great, she would not want someone in her apartment complex to see that car pull up in her parking lot and the driver going to her apartment. Donna said that her neighbors would assume that she had either called to report another person for hurting their children or that she herself was in trouble for hurting her own children. She feared that neighbors would believe that a visit from the agency meant that she was receiving some form of court-mandated programming as punishment for wrongdoing.

Susan was stunned by Donna's response because, as a CEO, she had never considered the perception of the vehicle logo. Susan might have thought that agency vehicles saved employees from using their own, that it was easier for tracking mileage, or that it was kind and convenient to arrive at someone's door rather than inconveniencing them with an office trip, and all of those thoughts make sense, but the key question is: Whose reality, whose perception, matters most?

I have shared this story in many different spaces and I usually get one of two reactions: vigorous nods and eye rolls, as if to say, "Duh! Of course, stakeholders think that!" or shock, as the CEO had, because they had never before considered that potential perception. This story further reinforces both the power of positionality, as we see only what we can based on our past and current experiences, and also how when our "great ideas" or standard practices touch real people, they can be wrong and require reconsideration. It also speaks to the power of the status quo and of leaders like Susan who often lean on the "this is the way we've always done it" thinking, which limits their ability to step back to get new perspectives.

Beyond the significant gaps in awareness and allegiance to accepted ways of problem-solving, we also forget that humans (yes, all of us) do not engage in solutions that do not make our lives easier and better. Just as you don't go to a store and buy everything in it, others also select items specifically suited for their needs, things that solve problems or increase pleasure. Even if there are other great products on the shelves, you prioritize what you need most and you dedicate the resources you have to best address your needs at that moment. Why would you buy something that doesn't help or that takes away your time, energy, and financial resources without providing benefit? You wouldn't. It is the same with programs, services, and interventions. For example, why would a stakeholder arrange and pay for childcare; drive, get a ride, or use public transport; miss work; push back their to-do list; delay rest; and/or increase stress to attend a meeting or program that does not provide immediate relief, resources, or support that will alleviate pain or improve their life? Stakeholders are not to blame in the slightest if they do not "take advantage of your support"; they are making the same decisions we all do.

## The Unrecognized Risk of Status Quo Problem-Solving Skills

In a sector that is so risk-averse (afraid of change, reluctant to explore new ideas, and adopt new practices, etc.), why do we use super risky problem-solving skills? The justification most offered for sticking with known ways to create change is that the sector is stewarding financial support that must be used responsibly and ethically to create the most benefit. And while it makes sense to protect investments, what is responsible and ethical about creating potentially weak impact and wasting massive amounts of financial and other resources using outdated skills?

The "giant triangle of waste" problem-solving model is not only hugely consumptive but also extremely risky for the organization's stakeholder relationships, resource investment, and reputation, mostly because of the assumptions made. Does the leader or decision-maker of the organization really know what stakeholders need and want? Is the solution the right one to create the most impact? Will a one-size-fits-all solution work or does the solution need to be modified or customized based on the different stakeholders impacted? These questions are only the tip of the assumptions iceberg. As sector professionals, we push forward using our outdated problem-solving habits, making assumptions without acknowledgment and testing. We are complicit in supporting these practices as a sector, and both funders and organizations are to blame for the waste caused by their ignorance and inattention.

I should note here that in the context of this book, I will use words such as "tests," "testing," and "hypothesis" usually in relation to Solution Testing, the fourth skill of the PAUSE framework. I want to acknowledge that words like these, while intended to confer the act of trying out different approaches to empower evidence-informed decisions, are also tainted by trauma and are connected to experimentation and the audacity of science and scientists to severely harm others, most often marginalized groups, in the service of "learning." My intent is to convey that we have options and pathways for learning that are enhanced by examining and trying out small actions that can provide early and important information to guide our next steps.

### The Funder's Role in Risk

Funders—by which I mean donors, foundations, impact investors, and government agencies that grant financial support— disincentivize risk in a few ways. First, funders love and expect

to see fully explained "giant triangles of waste." In grant proposals and pitches, they want you to predict the future and
show how, with your eloquent promises and plans for impact,
you can best provide *them* the assurance of certainty. Most
funders themselves use status quo problem-solving skills, so
they expect you to do the same.

Further, funders disincentivize risk when they require
lengthy applications and reports that may not always show-
case reality or the organization's ability to create impact. Most
really good proposals and reports often better reflect an organization's capacity to hire a great grant writer or marketing
expert than their ability to do great work. Nonprofits show and
share what worked, usually with tidy stories and charts. They
know they can't really share *everything* that happens behind
the curtain (and believe me, there is so much that never
reaches beyond the walls of most organizations) because
they will risk the loss of funding. As of now, the sector has not
widely adopted the enormous value of safely sharing learning,
iteration, and pivots, so we rely on outward representations of
seemingly all positive results.

Next, funders stunt risk with their beloved wait-and-see
approach. Many funders want to wait to see how new models, programs, and leaders will perform, and they often
require other funders to buy in before they will. As they wait,
organizations, ideas, and potential progress suffer, and the
riskier and newer a proposal feels, the more it is placed in the
wait-and-see category. If the majority of funders adopt this
approach, it is no surprise that large, established organizations that replicate the status quo receive the lion's share of
financial support. Where is there room for new, innovative,
grassroots-led organizations that are often more creative,
closer to the pain, and BIPOC-led?

Funders wield their power around risk in ways that are also
unfair. I have witnessed how funders talk to one another and

share missteps of organizations as a way to dissuade other funders from investing in them. While there is a time and place for holding organizations accountable for fiduciary and ethical violations, many organizations that do step out to try something new or that are transparent about what aspects go unexpectedly awry are "outed" and characterized as being a risky bet or less fundable. The information is often shared and received by another funder as an appreciated heads-up. I can guess this happens in every community, and it is frightening.

Last, there is also an interesting dynamic where certain funders say they want risky and dynamic proposals but then when the call is answered, they are either disappointed or become fearful and retreat. For example, I was working with a small community foundation and they put out a call for "innovative proposals." In year one, they received a small batch of submissions, and they were terribly disappointed. The foundation staff said things like, "These are similar to the proposals we usually get. Maybe our community doesn't know how to think in bold, innovative ways." They opened up the same mechanism in year two and received a stack of proposals with bold and innovative ideas. Their response in year two? "This feels a bit too out there," and "How would they actually pull this off?" This example illustrates the power that funders hold in this dynamic between organizations trying to meet undefined goals and parameters of "innovation" and funders not matching their risk talk with their risk walk.

### The Organization's Role in Risk

Funders' punitive behaviors and risk avoidance have trained organizations to avoid risk and bury failure, resulting in massive amounts of waste. One way this shows up is as a bizarre expectation and representation of perfection. Organizations play funders' perfection game by writing grant proposals and making promises to funders as if they can predict the future.

They say things like, "We will create X program, it will serve Y people, in Z months, and it will create these A, B, C forms of measurable impact," but do they really know any of that?

I like to explain the expectation of perfection and denial of failure by talking about science. Imagine a scientist sitting in a laboratory, surrounded by chemicals and other solutions that are contaminant-free and highly controlled. With such care and precision, how many times do their experiments go as expected the very first time? Almost never, right? They nearly always have to tweak an amount, a setting, a hypothesis. But somehow, we as a sector are expected to get our solutions right the very first time. This sounds even more ridiculous when we acknowledge that we're working with human beings who are infinitely complex, and we are operating in a space to address systems, structures, and practices that in many cases have been intentionally designed for hundreds of years to limit the possibilities and success of huge segments of our population. How does this make any sense, and why don't we acknowledge that we, too, are testing hypotheses, and we need the skills, resources, and flexibility to test them?

Another way risk shows up on the organization side of the sector is through competition (although funders do also compete in their own ways). The sector has fully bought into the idea of scarcity and that there's only so much proverbial pie to go around. Organizations continually operate in "not enough" mode and are expected to try to make the best of their limited resources and create (and evaluate) the most impact possible. If you match the dire and constant warnings of depleting dollars with the large number of existing and newly emerging organizations also vying for this limited funding, you get a paralyzing hot mess of fear and competition.

Because organizations believe they are operating in extreme austerity, it is even more imperative for them to hide missteps not only from funders but also from each other. They most definitely don't want other competing organizations in their community to learn about their issues, as it would show weakness and could impact their competitive advantage. We rarely like to acknowledge the competitive nature of the sector, but it is beyond real, and competition is another dynamic that funders have created and now sustain with their flawed grantmaking structures.

One story I encountered on my journey will forever make me sick to my stomach. I was working with a coalition of organizations from one community that was working on a shared mission of supporting families. One day, a few of the team members told me about issues they were seeing among some of their sister agencies. They said two different agencies that served nearly the same area of town were competing for "clients." One organization had the capacity to support community members, but they weren't able to fill their open spots. As a result, they had less than satisfying reports to share with their funders and financial support was waning.

The other organization was over capacity. They had a waiting list and were not able to support everyone who contacted them. Rather than reaching out to the other agency and referring people to them, they were using this increased demand to their advantage and had tweaked their funding solicitations to use the language, "For every one community member we support, three more are waiting for services. Please help now." Their donations were increasing and they were still struggling to meet the need.

If you examine these two experiences in isolation, you might say about the first organization, "Ah well, I guess there isn't room for everyone in this community, and organizations that support fewer people should go by the wayside." You might say about the second organization, "Wow! They are doing really great work and they need more help to meet demand. Let's make a gift!" As you can see in this example, which is sadly probably not totally unique, some organizations are prepared to gamble with and neglect human needs in order to retain their position, power, and privilege.

Can you imagine what would happen if organizations could have trust-based relationships with their funders, board members, staff, and communities? What if they could be vulnerable, share where their plans had to diverge, or when their logic model was off? What if the unexpected wasn't seen as failure but as lessons to be shared? What if these stories could be collected and shared across the sector?

Wouldn't it be awesome if there was an open-source searchable database in which you could enter the idea you were having, say, "community garden," and up would pop a treasure trove of learning? People could share what they had planned, what worked and what didn't (and why), and what advice they would offer to others just starting on their journeys.

One day I would love to create an open-sourced learning database, but for now, in every community, organizations are literally working on the same missions, building and operating essentially the same programs, and they are not only not talking to one another but also actively *hiding* information from each other. How does that make sense if we are to make progress on awful and persistent social problems? *The sector's fears of risk and retribution and the dynamics of expected perfection and competition are hamstringing us and stalling progress and possibility.*

## Organizations and Funders
## Both Rely on Good Intentions

I'm making the assumptions that, like me, you got into social impact work to make a difference, and that you care deeply about your calling and the communities you support. I would hope that as a sector, with every program we design and project we fund, our ultimate vision is to support people and transform their lives. We are not in this work to do damage, intentionally or unintentionally. Unfortunately, though, our sector does create harm, distrust, fear, unnecessary obstacles, and disappointment. While we may not intend to do harm, our intentions can predict only so much of what the outcomes may be. As Antionette Carroll, president and CEO of Creative Reaction Lab (creativereactionlab.com), and others are now emphasizing, intentions don't cut it and we have to focus on *impact*.

Even though our sector is fueled by good intentions, it doesn't mean that we get a free pass; our desire to do good does not cancel out what we put into the world. In other words, our perceived altruism and positive intent do not absolve us from taking responsibility and being held accountable for how we treat each other internally and externally and for the outcomes we create.

Related to favoring intent over impact, we often build and fund what *we* think "should" work. In the sector, we have very smart professionals and we've gotten pretty skilled at putting together those plans, charts, and models for how our programs will address a problem. While some rare organizations and programs will luck out and have success on their first try, just as designed, many programs will not create the most potential impact. We wouldn't intentionally design or fund programs that we thought wouldn't work, and our plans usually make logical sense, but as I've shared, I've seen so many projects go sideways once the solution implementation begins.

Funders also play a significant role in this dynamic of paying for what *they* think "should" work. Board and committee members have the power to decide which programs they deem most feasible and that they think will be successful. Their intent of providing community support is good, but their intent is essentially meaningless if the impact they choose to fund is not valuable or, in the worst case, is harmful.

Here are three examples of how what we think should be great can be wrong or harmful.

I was working with a department that had a new leader. Let's call him Michael. This director arrived with not only a lot of professional experience but also a lot of passion for making improvements. Michael saw an opportunity to streamline a process he thought would save resources and create a more positive experience for people accessing services. Sounds good, right? To kick off the change, he issued a description of the plan, including new workflows, and training began. He was very pleased with the new changes, and his boss was impressed with his focus on improving efficiency. Still sounds pretty good, right?

I thought so too until I talked to frontline staff. They were pissed. One staff member described in detail how the new workflows made his already taxing job three times harder. To most of the staff, the changes did not make sense and added unnecessary waste and steps. Staff were irritated that Michael, for whom they'd had so much hope as a new leader, had overlooked them and their perspectives before creating a change to which they were now held accountable. The feelings of disrespect and exclusion strained a department that already struggled with low morale and employee retention. Due to the hierarchically low positions of frontline staff and their lack of access to leadership, along with their fear of speaking out, the negative ripple of the change was not communicated outside of the frontline team.

Michael also never interacted directly with the community to make these changes. His intent was good; he was focused on improving a process, but because he trusted only his own perspective and fell into the trap of "the giant triangle," the unintended impact was extremely negative and harmful to the organization, and potentially the community.

Now I want to tell a story of one of the most memorable organizations I've had the honor of supporting. In one of the very first events I ever hosted, I offered training to a cohort of organizations in one community. One of the nonprofits was a very small organization that had a board member who was a retired executive and avid gardener. This board member, whom I'll call Alexandra, believed that the community needed more fresh fruits and vegetables to supplement their diets and the food they received from the food assistance boxes, so she wanted to start a community garden.

Alexandra had filled a massive binder in which she had tracked more than seven hundred hours of volunteer time she had committed to the project. She got land donated by the local government and had designed crop rotation and volunteer schedules; she was all in. The problem was that Alexandra was now asking for a budget, but the executive director, Syd, did not believe the program was necessary. In order to more deeply engage Alexandra in hearing feedback from the community, the director asked her to join their staff team at the training I was leading.

Within hours of talking to several community members, Syd got a very clear indication that people actually *did* have access to a variety of healthy foods and they did not express a need. Even though Alexandra participated in these conversations, she was undeterred and wanted to forge ahead. The team decided to investigate another aspect of the challenge that would be involved in recruiting a large number of garden volunteers. As a board member, Alexandra was very well connected, and she sent an email to her network as a quick test to see how many of her family, friends, and colleagues would offer to volunteer for this effort. She received a fantastic response—something like eighty positive email responses—and was bolstered further. I encouraged her to make her ask a bit more difficult to satisfy in order to test the extent to which people would really show up to help.

The next test was to ask those who responded to her email to attend an information session where they would choose their volunteer role. Unfortunately, only three of the eighty enthusiastic people showed up to that meeting. With the feedback from community members and the response from the meeting, Alexandra realized that she really was the only one convinced of the value of this project. She asked for a private meeting with me after the event and cried with remorse over all of the drained energy and distraction she had caused. To save face, she decided to leave as a board member.

Although it was a painful learning journey for Alexandra, Syd felt empowered. In the future, when a person with "a great idea" asked them to consider a new offering, they could now invite that person to apply the PAUSE framework *with them* to ensure that they were using their resources for the most impactful use. This invitation to learn with the organization now deepens respect for the leader and scares away those who "just have the ideas" and no energy for learning.

Another time, I was working with a department of an organization that was focused on supporting small business owners—in this case, restaurants. The organization had federal dollars they were considering granting to local restaurants for facade improvements. They assumed this would help the restaurants attract more diners. Their other intent was to create a more attractive main street that would stand out with new colorful awnings, fresh coats of paint, and other beautifications. Sounds snazzy and makes sense, right?

Thankfully, the team was not operating in "giant triangle of waste" mode and was using the PAUSE skills. As part of the process, the team interviewed restaurant owners. They were totally surprised when the owners, nearly unanimously, said they would prefer to use the money to upgrade their *interiors*. When the team dug deeper and asked why, the restaurant owners said that with Yelp, social media, and all the photos people were taking of their food, they would rather improve the look of the space inside, their menus, and the quality of their plates, silverware, and table decor so they would appear more attractive online.

The team thankfully began their process by talking to the restaurant owners first (they gathered these major insights in a matter of hours) and no harm and waste were caused. Can you imagine if the organization had just issued a program for exterior improvements without talking to the restaurant owners?

## PAUSE AND CONSIDER

**BEFORE I CAME** to this work, I used to build "giant triangles of waste." I remember feeling excited about "my" solutions. I loved the process of creation, and I even enjoyed the thrill and nervousness of the launch. What was less fun was experiencing the mismatch between the joy I felt while creating and the lack of impact that at times resulted from some of those programs.

Take a few minutes to answer these questions.

- How have you seen good intentions show up in your work?

- Have you ever created a solution that resembled the "giant triangle of waste"? What elements of the triangle resonate most and least with your experiences?

- Have you ever designed or been part of implementing a solution that did not create the intended impact? What happened? How did you feel? How did you respond and how did your organization respond?

- What has your experience been relating to risk in the sector? Where have you seen manifestations of the sector being risk-averse?

- What has your and your organization's experience been with taking risks?

# Why It's So Easy to Perpetuate the Status Quo

I T'S NO shocker that most of us, if given the choice between disrupting how we work and reaching into the unknown and staying cozy with what we know and what feels familiar, would choose comfort. If we are rewarded for sticking with the usual, we have even fewer reasons to branch out.

People and organizations want to create social change and positively impact stakeholders' lives. People want to feel like their work matters, and they are doing their best to be innovative, meet the need, stay competitive, and keep employees engaged and leaders effective. But honestly, our sector is using outdated means to reach these goals, given the complexity of this time and an even more unpredictable future. I like to lean toward the more positive view that people don't know what else to do, so they just keep marching forward. But at some point, our society will require additional interrogation of our status quo systems, practices, and outcomes. There are a few common pillars of our sector that we view as normal and acceptable but are, in fact, potentially problematic and wasteful.

## We Love "Best Practices"

As a sector, we want to use strategies and methods that have been tested, packaged, and proven to work. We also want uniformity and shared ways that we create change. This all makes sense, but I want to go deeper and get specific about the harm that "best practices" can potentially create. Let's walk through a few common needs in the nonprofit sector that most organizations seek guidance on and that are full of best practice recommendations.

Think about the scaffolding of training, advice, and support around how to create a new nonprofit. There are clear strategies for how to get started. If you need to secure funding, there is a plethora of professionals and strategies to help fill your bank account. Have a board? There are ways to make them and their meetings run more smoothly. Are you starting a philanthropic foundation? There are methods to establish your grantmaking processes. I can almost guarantee that if I plopped into a variety of local Association of Fundraising Professionals meetings or a variety of local grantmakers forums around the United States, I would hear very similar advice, tactics, and how-tos.

Using best practices and standard practices is highly regarded and supported; organizations *want* to use established methods, and funders *want* to fund their use. It makes logical sense that something that has won awards, been published, or used for years and years would have all the kinks worked out. Unfortunately, best practices are at times simply another form of the illusion of certainty.

There are a few elements of best practices that are problematic and a few ways we should interrogate their power. The first set of questions I recommend we ask as a sector are: Who says these are best practices? Who created them? Where did they come from? When were they created? We seem to accept so much of how we operate as a given and we rarely pause to consider the history, original source, and context of a multitude of practices that touch many of the core functions of our organizations, including program design, evaluation, fundraising, and board development.

The next question I would ask is: For whom are these best practices? What I have learned from connecting with more diverse people (people of color, disabled, LGBTQ2+, neurodivergent, and more) and non-US-based people who work in social impact is that there are multiple perspectives on how our work should be conducted, but those that deviate rarely make it to center stage. Best practices in the sector are widely based on white-dominant American norms and often do not accommodate and appreciate other forms of thought, expression, or action. Our existing best practices are often positioned as best for all when there is very clear evidence that they don't work for all.

The very act of calling something a best practice places it on a pedestal. It makes an approach feel defined, all buttoned up, and untouchable. In the sector, challenges to best practices are often dismissed or actively labeled as radical, harmful, and divisive. One example of this is Community-Centric Fundraising, a community of sector professionals who are bringing the deeper questions of equity, access, and power to the forefront of our work. If we are a sector intent on doing good, we must find strategies that do good for all.

It seems obvious, but there is another element of best practices that is rarely questioned: *Not every solution works everywhere and for everyone.* A solution that works well in Texas may not work well in New York, Oregon, or Wyoming. A solution that worked well with one stakeholder group may not work with another group—even a very similar group in another location. It is essential to ask, Will the best practice work well in my community as is? Since there is massive variation in local contexts, cultures, and histories, you must question and test best practices in *your* community, because chances are the solution is not as one-size-fits-all as it purports to be.

Last, sometimes when we accept and adopt best practices, we don't know the story *behind* them, and we take the promise of impact at face value. Here is one of my favorite stories from one of my all-time favorite clients to illustrate the challenge of adoption without interrogation.

My client was a city that was inspired by an award-winning program created by a nearby city to address the mental health issue of hoarding. The impetus for the program was the tragic death of a resident who had been unable to escape a house fire because they had been trapped by their belongings. Of course, my client's leadership did not want this to ever happen to one of their community members, so their plan was to "copy and paste" this program for use in their own city boundaries. After all, the program had won awards and been around for a few years, so it was super enticing and seemed like a no-brainer to implement.

Normally, when my client was interested in creating something new, they would initiate an exploratory process that included creating a twenty-person task force, budgeting about $100,000, and setting aside about ten months for research and recommendations. Thankfully, the assistant city manager at the time was intrigued by the "fail fast" mentality of start-up culture and wanted to try a new innovative approach to be more efficient and effective in setting up a new program. Before diving into adoption, the city manager decided to learn more about hoarding in *their* city.

They recruited a small team of four committed and amazing individuals (after a decade, still some of my favorite humans), and they started talking to all of the stakeholders potentially impacted by hoarding. These stakeholders included first responders; meter readers; staff working in permitting and planning, the county mental health agency, and housing-related social service agencies; and people experiencing hoarding. From these many chats, which took place over a few weeks, they learned some very interesting information. They learned that:

1   First responders, who included police, fire, and paramedics, did not have a sense of the true number of cases of hoarding they had seen because there was no system or expectation for tracking. Since there was no database or paperwork, and there were no other tracking tools, everyone was relying on anecdotal evidence and stories.

2   First responders were extremely overwhelmed by issues that they experienced as abundantly more pressing than hoarding, such as crime, injuries, and property-related offenses, and hoarding was not seen as a high priority.

3   The two above points were echoed in conversations the team had with other staff such as meter readers and permitting and planning officials in terms of the low priority of hoarding in their daily work, and lack of tracking other than a few anecdotal accounts that gave no insight into the scale of the problem.

4   The team learned from their local county mental health agency that the clinical diagnosis of hoarding had only just been recently added to the diagnostic manual and that the reimbursement codes for insurance had not yet caught up. This resulted in essentially a hoarding of hoarding cases by the county. No one knew until this interview that the

county was collecting contact information but providing zero support or treatment to individuals and their family members who reached out for help.

5  In the most kind and compassionate ways possible, the team members also attempted to interview people in the community who were experiencing hoarding. One individual they contacted had previously been provided extensive support from the city to clean their yard and home, and upon visiting, the team observed that the home had returned to its previous state, and the homeowner refused to talk to them. Each additional individual they approached declined to be interviewed and asked the team member to leave their property.

As you can imagine, the team felt very dejected and distressed that they were not getting traction for the project. In desperation and curiosity, they reached out to the award-winning city to ask about the secrets to their success and to share what they were learning. The person they talked to was kind and vulnerable enough to share (upon the promise of anonymity and a strong warning of "but you cannot tell anyone!") that the program they had spent years and millions of dollars to create did not work. They shared that all the data points the team had uncovered in their interviews were exactly the obstacles that prevented their own progress, primarily that first responders and other community partners were not engaged, and that individuals experiencing hoarding were refusing support.

When the team wrapped up the interview, they were shocked by the difference between what they had seen and heard about this program (the bright and shiny website, brochures, polished award acceptance speech at a conference) and the real talk that this person had shared. And while the team was still bummed that impact was to remain a distant promise, they were also thrilled to see that they were not alone in their learning and that they had accumulated the same amount of learning (or more) with a tiny team in just six weeks for the cost of about $6,000.

The team decided they had organized the evidence necessary to share their findings and recommendations with city leaders and their colleagues. They were terrified to present their findings and worried that they would be seen as failures who didn't have a "tied up with a bow" program to offer. With shaky voices and nervous stomachs, they recommended that 1) the city create an easy-to-use tracking form for all stakeholders to document and track cases of hoarding to get a sense of the number of cases, 2) a deeper exploration be conducted with the county mental health agency to address the backlog of hoarding cases, and 3) the city suspend implementation of the program.

As they waited for questions and comments following their presentation, the assistant city manager applauded their work and expressed their delight and appreciation for all of the time, money, and resources the team had saved the city. Rather than initiating a multiyear process of new program implementation at a cost of at least hundreds of thousands of dollars, the team had collected compelling evidence in a tiny fraction of the time and at a tiny fraction of the cost. This early experience has created a long relationship that has saved the city millions of dollars by not building solutions that stakeholders do not want. For other challenges, in a matter of weeks, teams learned how to implement powerful solutions with evidence and validation.

Unfortunately, and frustratingly, this team's experience of uncovering the reality behind a "best practice" is not the only one I have witnessed. In fact, I've had this exact experience numerous times, in the form of these same sorts of interviews during which teams uncover that a bright and shiny program is actually a hot mess—and I've seen it more intimately too. I've known multiple organizations that were very comfortable presenting their frameworks at conferences and fully accepting recognition for their "success," some even winning pitch competitions, while back at the office they had hired me to "fix" or figure out why their program was not working. This is yet again a manifestation of the fear and risk of being exposed to our funders and to each other, and unfortunately, it has created a rarely recognized ugly underbelly of our work in the sector.

This section is not to suggest that you approach and treat every best practice like snake oil or a deceptive offering, but you should adopt a curious mindset and be an informed consumer. Before you adopt a new best practice, one of the most useful things you can do is interview the creator (or provider) of the best practice as well as those who have used the methodology in their organization. Here are some of my favorite questions to ask:

- What's your favorite part of using the practice? What's working?

- What's the most challenging part of using the practice? What's not working?

- If you could start again, is there anything you would change or do differently?

- What would you recommend for someone like me who is just considering using the practice?

My teams have asked these questions of best practice programs, and I have connected past clients to prospective clients to have a chat about my own framework. It is always extremely enlightening to understand more deeply how a framework functions in real life. What we see presented on conference stages, in articles, and on websites is the best outward-facing representation of what has been created, and when we have access to the fullness of the framework, the pros *and* cons, we can make fully informed decisions about its adoption.

## We Wait for Results

The discussion of results and metrics in the sector is a tricky one. We have significant issues in evaluation, such as the lack of equitable and antiracist evaluation design, weak recognition of the power of both qualitative *and* quantitative evaluation, and an absolute misalignment of expectations between funders and the realities and complexities of supporting communities, all while most organizations have no data collection and data analysis funding or expertise. The hoops we jump through are painful, and when we are given one to three years of usually restricted funding to make a demonstrable and significant impact on a difficult social problem, it becomes pretty absurd.

But with that said, we also are missing a key piece of *early* testing and validation. While I recognize that making an impact on social issues at times takes decades and generations, we lack the skills to get early validation for our ideas. For a sector driven by urgency to address community needs, we seem to be satisfied waiting for months and years to gather, examine, and share the results of our interventions.

We are so used to building our "giant triangles of waste"— doing research, choosing a solution, and preparing and perfecting our implementation plans (usually to comply with expectations of funders, executive leaders, and board members)—that we don't even recognize that there must be a better way to test potential solutions. In fact, most traditional and status quo evaluation is based on the same "giant triangle of waste" and jointly sits upon a massive amount of unrecognized and untested assumptions. The goals, objectives, timelines, and short- and long-term metrics are often all tied to untested strategies and assumptions about what we think should work, how, for whom, and by when.

We often think that conducting pilot studies will give us "quick" results because we just have to fund or run one year of a project and then "see what happens," but in my experience, even just one year of funding can often be a waste of resources. When teams use the PAUSE framework, they can get an indication in as little as thirty minutes (the time it can take to run one rapid test) whether a program should be explored or left behind. I have also seen teams uncover in a matter of hours amazing opportunities to add value to a program that they never even had on their radars and that can be immediately integrated into the overall program design.

Let me share one of my favorite examples of what can happen when we use status quo problem-solving skills and wait to see results. A foundation hired me to help them figure out why a program they had funded for three years, for the cost of about a half-million dollars, had served only a few hundred community members. This project was a collaborative effort involving multiple hospitals, health clinics, and community agencies to support individuals who were released from the hospital and had no support network at home. This means that people who were discharged from the hospital were going to be home alone with no one to do things like pick up their medications, do their grocery shopping, or take them to follow-up appointments. Not surprisingly, local data showed that community members without these forms of support had elevated rates of reinjury and rehospitalization. The program was initiated because the lead nonprofit had seen a best-practice program in another community.

From what I could gather after coming onto the scene in year three, the funder had received reports that reflected the lower numbers of community members served but had been promised that new strategies and methods were coming to resuscitate the program. The staff responsible for this program were deeply connected to the problem and the community members impacted, and they tried *everything* to breathe life into this work.

The design for the program was logical—the goal was to connect caring volunteers to community members being discharged via referrals by their medical partners. In year one, it seemed like everyone was optimistic, living up to what they promised in the Memorandums of Understanding (MOUs), and they were well informed about the project. In year two, the lead agency was seeing fewer and fewer referrals, even after trying to make some tweaks in their outreach and collaboration strategies. Year two also included some staff and leadership changes and people seemed to deprioritize the program. By year three, the lead agency and funder were still not seeing the traction they wanted, partners were ignoring each other's calls, and staff at one of the medical sites were downright hostile when the lead agency attempted to re-engage their interest in the program.

I was brought in to diagnose and try to fix what was happening when the funder was considering what to do next, either continue funding or end support. I formed two teams of representatives across the various partner agencies. The teams set out over two days to understand and determine the root cause of the lack of enrollment and participation and how they might collectively rectify the issues. Within the first six hours on the first day of training, they identified a massive missed opportunity that no one had ever addressed in three years of work: No one had ever talked to the case managers who were responsible for making the program referrals at the medical facilities. During the early stages of the work, no one thought to identify key stakeholders beyond the three main ones impacted: people being discharged from the hospital, the volunteers, and the medical partners. It turns out that the referral staff were the most important in the entire intervention.

You might read that and think, "Duh! What the heck!?" but I can tell you story after story of when an intervention or program was created and the people most key to the program were never included. (My "favorite" being the multimillion-dollar volunteer center that when designed never included volunteer input, but I digress . . .)

When the team interviewed the referral staff, so much became clear. The team learned that staff's work lives were very hectic and so jam-packed that they barely had time to focus on anything beyond emptying beds and connecting with new patients. We also learned that none of the case managers knew about the program because turnover was very high in that role and there was no method for training new staff to learn about the program when they were hired. This was all new information to the team members in terms of the direct impact to their shared program and outcomes.

Once we better understood the referral staff, we identified gaps in our understanding of the medical partners (CEOs of hospitals, directors of clinics, etc.) as key stakeholders. To provide a buffer between these leaders and the teams, I personally interviewed representatives from each site, and what I learned was surprising and sad. Most shared with me what they were too nervous or polite to share with the lead agency—that they didn't believe the program actually worked, and some felt the program didn't have the right volunteers in place to connect with the patients they were discharging.

When I shared my learning from the medical partners with the lead agency, the staff were stunned and angry. These beliefs and assumptions had never been shared with them over the three years, and they believed them to be false. They felt that patients who were supported by the program *did* have improved outcomes and they *had* worked to increase their variety of volunteers who were bilingual and willing to travel to all parts of the community. Due to fear of having courageous and sensitive conversations, a huge divide had grown between the collaborative partners.

The lack of communication with referral staff and the project leaders took its toll. When the team tried to offer training to referral staff, few showed up. When the team re-engaged with the clinic and hospital leaders and tried to pivot the recruitment model to include posters placed in pre-surgery, admission, and recovery rooms, with the intent that patients themselves would call to enroll in the program, the lead nonprofit agency and funder still did not see the results they wanted.

The funder took all of the learning into consideration and, after providing a bit of short-term funding to continue additional tests, decided to end support for the program. The project left me feeling so sad for two reasons. First, I saw the anguish, defeat, and frustration of the lead agency staff who had weathered the stress of communicating with the funder, partners, patients, and volunteers. They tried so hard for years but felt like they were fighting an uphill battle, without knowing why. What makes me the saddest is my assumption that if the program had been codesigned from the beginning to optimize value for *all* stakeholders to create trust, authentic collaboration, and open communication, potentially more community members could have been helped, and perhaps the program learning could have led to other support programs.

In this example, and in the example about individuals experiencing hoarding, and so many others you will read in the chapters ahead, we have a serious gap in knowledge about how to test potential solutions before we implement, and because the "give it twelve months" standard is so widely adopted, we cannot see beyond our normal practices. Waiting for results not only robs organizations of early potential impact and learning but also consumes hundreds of hours and thousands of dollars tied up in potential solutions that may not create the greatest impact. I've shared just a few examples, but consider the amount of time, energy, and resources we waste as a sector collectively while we wait for results.

## We Are Challenged by Complexity

When I was early in my entrepreneurial and consulting career, new, small, and growing organizations were some of my favorite types of clients to support. I especially loved working with organizations that were learning a new skill for the first time. I used to feel very confident saying things like, "Okay, here's how you fundraise," "Here's what to consider when recruiting board members," and "Here's how grant writing works."

When I was new to fundraising, I was learning from many seasoned and recognized professionals in the field, and I accepted strategies without question. Like many, I did not grow up thinking my career would include fundraising, but once I was developing and designing programs, my organizations needed cash to bring them to reality, and I began to learn how it all worked. What I learned was that there are very specific methods and recommendations for how you identify and research potential donors, communicate with donors, and cultivate and steward gifts. As I heard the same messages over and over again, I thought, "I guess this is how it works and this is what I have to do to be successful."

As time went on and as I put more of these strategies into practice and taught others to use them, a strange and unexpected thing happened. Contrary to what you would expect, as I worked with more and more clients, I got *less and less* confident sharing these "this is how it's done" tips and tricks. With a lot of guilt and shame, my thoughts began to shift to include, "I feel like something is missing," "Is this really all we have as a sector, this repetitively spewed set of strategies?" and "This doesn't feel like it jibes 100 percent." I began to dislike the dynamics that surround some of the core pillars of the sector, and I wondered why we accepted some of the practices that felt inherently inauthentic, inequitable, and ineffective. In my naivete, what I thought was replicable and straightforward was anything but, and full of tensions and intersectional and systemic dynamics.

For example, people might say that some fundraising strategies (direct mail, events, email and social media outreach, wealth mapping, one-on-one solicitation, case statements, annual reports, etc.) have stayed around because they work, but I would argue that maybe they've also stuck around because very few people have challenged how they work and haven't been made to. We are currently questioning so much that is and has been accepted in our society, and the sector is not immune.

Let's consider fundraising again. We say that fundraising is asking someone to make an investment in our mission, but it is much more complex. Fundraising also involves love, power, privilege, compassion, wonky relationships with money, family legacy, racism, hope, extraction, capitalism, inspiration, joy, patriarchy, stories and narratives (true *and* false), relationship building, wealth and wealth-hoarding, healing, human kindness, corruption, the historical and current ways that wealth was and is made in this country, liberation, taxes and tax evasion, lies, transformation, broken systems and structures, and more. Not so simple.

As a sector, we need to flow in the tension that is complexity. Our work is about love *and* control, compassion *and* harm, and we must give the current and next generation of sector professionals permission to look beyond the tidy handbooks of "this is how this work is done" and acknowledge that these "best practices" can only get us so far. What if we had new practices that accounted for complexity, change, and multiple worldviews?

## PAUSE AND CONSIDER

**WE WORK** so hard in the sector, and most of us really care about our colleagues and communities. It is a shame that the guardrails that dictate our work, the expectations, and the "ways it's done" can unintentionally derail and undermine our ability to create greater and more meaningful impact and reach fulfillment as individuals and as a sector. In the "busyness" of all we do, it is imperative that we all take time to pause and consider ways that our work does and does not align, and to explore what might be possible if we noticed, questioned, and acted differently. Consider these questions:

- Are there ways that you or your organization have researched, copied, and/or implemented a best practice program? If yes, how did you learn about it? Were you able to test strategies or talk to anyone prior to implementation?

- Have you ever felt that the work you were doing, following a "this is the way it's done" model, was missing something? What specifically were you working on, and what questions did you have? What gaps, needs, and incongruities did you notice?

- How do you and your organization measure results? Do you use pilot programs? If so, how long do those projects usually have to demonstrate results? How successful are those pilots?

# TWO

## HOW DO WE MAKE CHANGE USING THE PAUSE SKILLS?

# What Do
# We Do Instead?

IN PART ONE, I talked about why our sector needs to reimagine how we address challenges and uncertainty. You've read about, and hopefully paused to consider more deeply, the issues of positionality, and holding the tension of working in the sector while acknowledging what needs to change. I hope you are seeing how our tangled relationships with risk, the "giant triangle of waste," "best practices," and our best intentions are missing the mark and can potentially create harm. While it's very important to spend time analyzing what's deficient and why, it is equally important to ask, "What can we do instead?"

What we can do first is pause. We can take a beat to be thoughtful, curious, and intentional. Pausing is powerful because it creates the space you need for "aha" moments and new action. There is nothing more exciting than watching light bulb moments, like when someone says, "I never thought of that before," "I didn't know that's what was going on or that people felt that way," "Wow, there is more to this," and then moving toward, "We can do better and make a difference."

## The Benefits of PAUSE-ing

Here are just some of the ways you and your organization benefit when you pause to work differently. You

- illuminate and reignite your passion and your power to learn, and expand what is possible;

- leverage diversity of perspectives and authentic teamwork;

- shift your organizational culture from doing to learning;

- connect with community in respectful and powerful co-creation;

- listen, observe, and gain game-changing insights;

- see value creation opportunities for internal and external stakeholders;

- see your potential solutions not as scarce and precious but as abundant and up for testing;

- choose evidence-informed next steps that democratize decision-making; and

- invest resources in what you know will address problems.

These are new problem-solving skills that you can use on your own and in teams across your organization and community. I hope you are saying to yourself, "That all sounds great!" *and* you may also be wondering, "So what does this 'instead' look like?" It looks like, in a matter of *hours, days, and weeks,* many organizations making more progress than they've had working on a challenge for multiple *years*. By twelve weeks, organizations have usually uncovered a significant amount of the breadth and depth of a challenge, and they often know what to build (or not) and why. Leaders are usually stunned by the level of advanced teamwork, accelerated learning, and the depth of root-cause insights achieved in such a short time. I want to briefly pause and address the references I make related to the speed of learning or the shortened time to certainty and evidence. This focus on rapidity is not intended to reinforce a major flaw of the social sector connected to urgency and rushing to create solutions and demonstrate results, but rather to illustrate that if individuals, teams, and organizations are provided dedicated time and coaching to learn and apply new skills, they can reach potential solutions much more efficiently and effectively. The multiday workshops that teams experience are intended to provide opportunities for practice, followed by weeks of intensive support to improve their skills, integrate new learning, and increase organizational support.

Some organizations save hundreds of thousands of dollars and countless resources and staff time *not* building solutions that nobody wants. Organizations that fast-track possibilities or discover solutions that were never on their radar have benefited from new revenue streams, angel investment, increased grant funding, improved retention, and increased recruitment. The majority of staff and organizations that have learned this approach are still using the skills years later and have advanced in their careers, been highlighted to speak about their success at conferences, referred others, and returned for more.

While there are so many different positive aspects of the PAUSE framework, I want to focus on the core of the work, and that is all about connection. *At its root, this work is about connecting to yourself and better understanding how you see the world. It's about connecting to colleagues and your team members to see them in the fullness of who they are. And it's about connecting to the community and the many stakeholders you support.*

This new way of learning also connects you more to your work so that you feel more aligned with your purpose, and you can see very quickly how the potential solutions you pursue and how you get to that learning really make a difference. I don't want to overstate or make an unrealistic and inauthentic promise that after you address one challenge, you will see instant and magical organization-wide transformation (which is often what leaders unrealistically expect), but I can guarantee that if you use this framework consistently, you personally will be changed. As you use the skills to address one and then multiple challenges, you will be committed because you will repeatedly experience the difference in how you feel doing your work, and you will continue to see immediate learning and impact. Many changemakers share that they now see how their old ways and skills were essentially wasteful and, at worst, harmful. I hope you, too, will see that you can start with you and then shift your culture to one of learning.

## Honoring the Struggle of Learning

While the benefits I just outlined are real, the journey is, of course, not all rainbows and butterflies. At first, working this way feels uncomfortable—and it should. I am proposing that you shift your habits, the ways you think and work, and fully embrace the unknown, which we know the brain and body don't appreciate. I like to think of it as if you are dusting away the cobwebs of the status quo solutions and skills you are used to applying to your work. It's very similar to that feeling of doing a good spring cleaning: You do the hard, dirty work of dragging out the old clothes, sorting through drawers and cabinets, and schlepping away your used items. After you're done, you feel lighter, you have more space literally and figuratively, and you may feel open to new possibilities. That end result, that feeling of potential, is how I want you to feel about this process.

To make space for learning, we must recognize that learning does not happen in a straight line. At its foundation, wanting (and believing in) a clean, linear path to information and impact reveals just how much most people have bought into status quo thinking about how individuals and organizations are expected to move forward, problem-solve, and create change. Wanting a straight line is totally normal and it's how we are taught in the dominant culture that things work. But in fact, it is a myth, and we need to let those beliefs and expectations go. We must recognize and accept that learning

- is winding, twisting, messy, unpredictable (and at its best, unexpected);

- takes time, patience, listening, flexibility, humility, empathy, compassion, and vulnerability;

- means getting out of your own thinking and silos;

- means letting go of what you think should happen;

- is not about plowing ahead to find validation, but, rather, intentionally naming and prioritizing the gaps in your learning; and

- means releasing agendas and biases and allowing all forms of "data" to guide your next steps.

Because the PAUSE framework is all about introducing you to new skills, it also means you need to embrace a new definition of success. *When you are navigating uncertainty, success is not about how quickly you can implement a solution; it is about embracing the learning journey and where it leads you.* Embracing a new definition of success means you accept that there are numerous possible outcomes and all are successful because they are built on efficient and effective learning.

Often, people will ask, "How do I know if I'm doing this 'right'?" and my answer is, "Did you learn something that you didn't know before?" This new way of working will challenge your existing thoughts and practices, and it requires both vulnerability and trust that learning will lead you to the outcomes you are meant to cocreate. Just as our brains and bodies aren't fans of uncertainty, being vulnerable is also not our favorite state. But as Brené Brown aptly shares, "Vulnerability is the birthplace of innovation, creativity, and change." We must be vulnerable and open enough to challenge our old beliefs and change our actions.

## We All Show Up Differently

When I began doing this work, I was pretty naïve. I used to arrive at a multiday client event with so much excitement, hope, and positive energy, and I assumed that everyone there felt the same way. I imagined that everyone was super thrilled and totally ready to hang out with me to shake up their thinking and actions.

I still arrive with excitement, hope, and positive energy, but that sweet, optimistic bubble burst pretty early. I quickly recognized that I needed to meet each person where they were and that people arrive with excitement and hope but also hesitation, skepticism, fear, and anger. Just because you begin this journey does not mean that you will love every part of it, that you will be met with total support, or that you will arrive at the outcomes you had in mind. You must recognize that you are also pausing in your current organizational culture, for better or for worse.

While the struggle is absolutely real and the work to create social change is hard, there is hope, and there are ways you can both acknowledge the space you're in *and* keep learning.

Amy Edmondson, Harvard Business School professor and author of seven books, talks about the Learning Zone. This is the zone where you feel safe and supported to say, "I don't know" and you have the flexibility to let the learning reveal what it may. In this zone, not only are you open to learning, but also you feel highly accountable for making progress on your challenges. It is also important to notice key barriers you might be constructing unintentionally that will prevent your optimal learning, such as resisting new information, letting the stress of your to-do list prevent you from seeing the big picture, or giving away your power by assuming that you need permission to learn and take action. When you notice you are slipping out of the Learning Zone or constructing these barriers, name them and let them pass so you can continue making progress.

## PAUSE Framework Goals

When I work with new clients, I say upfront and very clearly that I do not have the answers or their solution. I do not know what is going to create the most value for stakeholders, and I do not know what will prove to be the most technically and outcomes feasible. I don't have a way to predict the future, but what I do tell people is that if they trust the PAUSE process, they will get to the answers they are seeking—and so will you.

This book is not meant to be a theoretical dive into how you might work differently. I want you to work through the book and apply the framework to a challenge you need to address. The multiple examples I share are meant to inspire you and validate what you might have also seen and felt in your work. One person working this way can absolutely make a difference. If you form a team around the work, even better. And when you begin to address multiple challenges across an organization, the real transformation begins. My greatest hope is that you will not only become adept at using the framework when in uncertainty, but also integrate these skills into your daily practice and reflection time in order to achieve personal growth.

In Part One of the book, we talked a lot about the "giant triangle of waste." I want you to keep that visual and its content top of mind as a cautionary reminder, but now that we've shifted to how to work differently, I want you to embrace the PAUSE skills, an acronym for each skill of the framework. I will dive into each element of the PAUSE framework and provide you with the "why," the how-to, and more Pause and Consider provocations. This book is written to support individuals and teams who want to integrate these new skills, and you will see where I go deeper in explaining how teams can share the work and their learning. I also have a lot of content that I could not include in the book (you didn't want to read five hundred pages, right?) so I have created handouts for tips, lessons, and more on my book website, NoMoreStatusQuoBook.com, that I encourage you to please check out. I will also indicate throughout how you can learn more and get additional support for specific steps of the PAUSE framework.

Rather than ending the problem-solving process with a grand reveal to our stakeholders, using new skills, we *begin* by cocreating with our stakeholders, and they are included at every step of the learning journey. We do not invest continual and ever-increasing resources in working toward the execution of our one solution, but we begin with a strong foundation built upon clarity and alignment, and we build in pause points for reflection and decision-making so that we can confine our investment to what makes the most sense and is driven by evidence. Instead of taking months and years, it can take just hours and weeks to gain immediate insights and provide you with increasing clarity, confidence, and learning. I am beyond excited for you to jump in and begin your learning journey!

**SOLUTIONS CODESIGNED WITH
STAKEHOLDERS AT EVERY STEP**

**EVIDENCE-INFORMED
DECISION-MAKING**
Communicate your
decision-making effectively

PAUSE

**SOLUTION TESTING**
Prioritize and
test potential solutions

PAUSE

**UNDERSTAND
STAKEHOLDERS**
Listen to the current needs
of stakeholders

PAUSE

**ASSESS UNCERTAINTY**
Identify blocks to your learning

PAUSE

**PACKAGE THE CHALLENGE**
Align before jumping to solutions

Stable foundation

**PLANNING + PROGRESS (Hours to Weeks)**
Clarity · Confidence · Learning

## PAUSE AND CONSIDER

I THINK the PAUSE framework is pretty sweet, *and* as I have acknowledged, learning and putting new skills into practice is full of tension and includes elements that you will both love and hate.

I hope you will trust the process and be self-aware about your evolving journey, how you begin, how it feels, what you need, what you are learning, and how it shifts you and your work. I also hope that while you can relate to the "giant triangle of waste," you see the benefits of these new skills so that you can work differently to save time and money, and uncover amazing potential solutions to support stakeholders.

As you begin this journey and put this framework into action, consider these questions:

- When I talk about "aha" and light bulb moments, can you think of recent examples of when you've had that experience in your work?

- Have you ever thought about how it *feels* to learn? Do you feel in your flow, open, expanded? Do you feel stressed, pushed out of your comfort zone, a bit too vulnerable? Both? It depends?

- When was the last time that learning felt easy, or when did you last feel like you were in the Learning Zone? Do you have any insight as to why you felt this way?

# Package the Challenge

PACKAGE THE Challenge is the "P" of the PAUSE skills and is the essential first step to creating a solid foundation for learning. Package the Challenge includes two parts: the first focuses on getting aligned with your challenge and stakeholder, and the second, on forming a team.

The three provocations that drive the first part of this skill include:

- What if we were aligned?
- What if we had clarity?
- What if we were informed?

It makes logical sense that before you head down a path, you know *why* you are going there and what you intend to explore. Unfortunately for many organizations, this "path," their challenge, stakeholders, and even their organization's mission, vision, values, programs, and metrics of success, are often murky, not well communicated, or interrogated.

I remember feeling uninformed, excluded, and misaligned as I sat through yet another poorly run staff meeting and asked, again, "Does what we are working on connect to our mission?" I got blank and frustrated stares, and while at times I was being a bit of an intentional troublemaker in such meetings, my intent was usually to push my colleagues to consider the same things so that *I* felt more purposeful, passionate, and connected.

Many people do not know basic information about the decisions or strategies that drive their work. As organizations get larger and more complex, silos and hierarchical structures emerge, information starts to break down as departments no longer collaborate or check in, and leaders, managers, and frontline staff do not have clear pathways to move information up or down, or across their organization. As organizations grow and get busier, there's also a lack of time and space that enables people to pause their execution work and think systematically and strategically.

The potential result is staff members who feel disconnected and frustrated, and, at worst, information becomes hoarded or weaponized by staff who restrict the flow of information to maintain power or control. Leaders will often restrict information flowing down because they don't believe they need to include anyone but their executive team or board members in their decision-making. I've worked with leaders who felt that engaging stakeholders would just create delays, cost too much, and open a "Pandora's box" of other issues, so they continued to avoid it. Other organizations had implemented super ineffective and inefficient attempts to share information across the entire organization (most often without staff feedback), usually in the form of painfully boring and wasteful meetings.

One of the hardest roles to be in, and one that can generate a lot of these disconnect issues, is that of middle manager. These poor souls are often stuck in a hierarchical communication and decision-making vise, where they feel pressure from above to deliver impact and pressure from below to share power and guidance. I'm guessing you've experienced some of these same challenges and more.

Unfortunately, the end result of these disconnects and dynamics can be a lack of learning and impact. I have seen with increasing frequency, especially in large, prominent organizations, that while on the outside they still have their polish and promise, inside, they have weak leadership and processes, and over time their staffing, programs, and impact slowly wither.

In my early client discovery work, I go deep with leaders and teams to understand their challenges and stakeholders because it is my first step toward uncovering all of the dynamics above. I'll often ask the following questions:

- What are the most challenging aspects of your work and your biggest areas of uncertainty?

- Are there any big changes, any disruptions within your organization that I need to know about?

- How are decisions made within your organization? Who has the power in terms of dictating strategy, program investment, employee engagement, etc.?

- How do you learn as an organization and as individuals? How is learning shared?

- Why do you think the challenge you have selected is important?

- What else have you tried to address this challenge? What has worked and what hasn't?

- Think of a time when you created something and it did not reach the desired result. What was your reaction? The organization's reaction? Was the negative or poor outcome analyzed (or was it swept under the rug)?

These conversations help give me an early peek behind the curtain and inform how I guide the specific focus for the organization.

## Picking the Challenge

If I asked you right now to name a challenge you need to address or perhaps an intriguing or exciting opportunity in your work or organization, could you name one? Most people can name at least one, and the goal of this step of the framework is to select a current project, process, or challenge area (internal or external) about which you and your organization would like to develop significant learning and ignite greater progress.

The top question prompts to consider when selecting a challenge include:

- What (and where) are significant pain points within your organization and/or in the community?

- What are the ways in which you are not achieving your vision and mission, or meeting your goals?

- Where are there high-priority gaps, missing pieces, and potential opportunities?

- Where is there uncertainty in your strategic priorities or key projects or initiatives?

- Where are there significant areas of wasted time, resources, energy, etc.?

- What are your aspirational goals (e.g., how do we offer a new, best, better _____)?

I've been exposed to numerous different types and sizes of organizations and different types and sizes of challenges, both addressing internal and external issues. Some challenges fall into common categories, and others are pretty specific. Some examples of projects I've supported include improving the onboarding experience for new employees, creating new ways to appreciate community volunteers, increasing community member recruitment or retention, redesigning community policing strategies, streamlining a grant management process, creating a nationwide program to improve gender parity, and increasing COVID-19 vaccine access and uptake by Latine and Native American communities.

One of the key questions to ask yourself when you are thinking about a challenge is whether it is an *execution* or a *search* challenge. I'm reluctant to use the word "or," as challenges usually fall somewhere on a spectrum, but in general, *execution* projects are those that are well understood. You might be making slight tweaks or improvements, and you can usually hold people accountable to metrics and timelines to complete the work. *Search* projects are those that are highly unknown—you are not sure how to best create value, you do not have clarity on how the solution should best function to create impact, and, therefore, you cannot assign timelines or metrics for accountability.

Examples of an execution project might include redesigning a brochure or website. The content should be tested with stakeholders and redesigned with feedback, but the factors to be considered are pretty well known. Examples of search projects might be driven by big unknowns and questions like, "How do we identify and support community leaders to extend our impact?" "How do we best engage families to sign up for and complete our programs?" and "How do we design engaging professional development?"

As I've said, the *search* versus *execution* question is a bit squishy, as some projects fall somewhere in between. Let's say your organization wants to update an internal process. The process already exists but you want to see what steps can be eliminated, determine who needs to be included and when, identify for whom the process creates the most bottlenecks, and more. There can be something existing within your work or organization that you want to tweak, but it can also be filled with unknowns.

Even though placing your challenge on this spectrum can be flexible, I bring up this differentiation and awareness of *execution* and *search* for three reasons. First, if your challenge is very well known, project management is often a better fit than using the PAUSE skills. The PAUSE skills were designed for helping people gain clarity on challenges that have uncertainty.

Second, it is very common and dangerous when all new tasks and projects are all treated as if they are *execution*. They get added into the "giant triangle of waste" process, and when this happens, staff most often are expected to adopt a project, conduct research, and create a plan by a deadline and adhere to metrics, when many times no one really knows what will best support stakeholders and create impact.

I once supported a group of city analysts revamping an internal process, and they shared with me that although "analysis" was in their title, they rarely had time to actually analyze the challenges they were given to solve and most often hastily pushed through a solution to meet leaders' expectations. They are not alone, and I've met staff for whom this way of working creates significant anxiety because they don't have the answers, yet are expected to deliver outcomes. It also reinforces the false belief that intent, planning, and progress equal impact, and I think I've already clearly established how this is wasteful thinking.

Third, because your challenge is uncertain, the first framing of your challenge and choice of a challenge might be off or need adjustment. Think of your challenge as your first hypothesis. I will show you as we proceed together all the considerations to make as you learn.

So, pause for a few moments here and think: What is your challenge?

## Choosing the Stakeholder Who "Matters" Most

You might read that heading and think, "Gah, how rude! Who *matters* most?! That is horrible!" I don't mean identifying the most valuable human or set of humans; this is about getting specific about *who is most impacted by your challenge.* Once you choose one challenge to begin with, it is important to next consider *all* of the stakeholders impacted by the challenge and choose one stakeholder group to focus on first.

What we often do using status quo problem-solving skills is hold the belief that one program will satisfy and solve a problem for every potential stakeholder. *We love one-size-fits-all solutions. They feel simple and clear, but essentially when we create one program, we often make it the job of the stakeholder to figure out where they fit in and where to find value.* This really does not make any sense, as programs and processes are intended to address problems and create value so that stakeholders will buy in, participate, and derive benefit. If we offer one solution for all, we have to question which people we are talking about, because rarely does one uniform solution create value for everyone.

Let's say your organization wants to increase fundraising dollars received from corporate partners. This challenge touches the communities you support; your board; executive leaders; development staff; program staff; evaluation team; volunteer managers; and, of course, your former, existing, and prospective corporate donors; the corporate social responsibility arm of a company; and employees of the company. Whew! As you can see, there are many stakeholders involved, and designing a strategy to simply "get more money from big businesses in town" is more complex than you might imagine.

The ways that you create value for external stakeholders—in this example, corporate partners—will vary based on many factors such as each business's mission, leadership, and giving priorities. The ways in which you might create value for internal stakeholders will also vary greatly. The things your volunteer management team need to codesign great corporate employee experiences that will engage new individual donors and volunteers to support your mission is very different from the value you create for your board members, whom you might ask to identify, meet with, and solicit business leaders they may know in their networks. Corporate partners', volunteer managers', and board members' needs, pain points, strategies, and desired outcomes are different. If you are not clear on *what* problem or need you are trying to address for someone, or a group of people, and specifically *how* you might address their needs, how can your outcomes be anything other than weak and unclear?

It is also important to acknowledge that within a specific group, there lies intradiversity. I once worked with an organization that supports foundations of all types and sizes across one state. They were seeing a decrease in their recruitment of new members and that existing members were disengaging. Moreover, an increasing number were not renewing their membership, leading to financial challenges for the organization. Their original idea was that they needed to rebrand, create a new logo, and redesign their collateral and website. Thankfully, they decided to delay that work and instead focus on getting to the root of their challenge. They affirmed very quickly that their members fit into different buckets based on their type of giving and their experience and expertise in grantmaking. For example, a large family foundation with decades of giving experience needed and wanted very different support from that of a new family foundation in its early formation stages; corporate foundations needed support that was different from that of foundations formed to address specific medical issues. They were able to rethink how they were currently marketing their services, which went from a "Here's what we do, come and get it!" approach to a message saying, "You are unique, and we have custom support for your needs now and into the future."

It may be frustrating to focus on just one stakeholder at a time because it feels like you don't have time for that level of focus, but in my experience, you don't have time *not* to be focused. When we don't focus, we risk creating wasteful services that don't directly address specific needs.

To choose one stakeholder on which to focus first, you need to make your own comprehensive list of who is connected to or impacted by your challenge, and be sure to consider stakeholders internal and external to your work and organization. Once you have what probably seems like a very overwhelming list, consider factors like who is feeling the most pain or frustration, who has the greatest need related to your challenge, and with whom you need to make the most significant impact first to really make sure that the program is creating value.

Again, this prioritization does not mean that you are saying that one group of individuals is more important or valuable than another; rather, you're acknowledging that you cannot solve a problem for every person at the same time. The good news is that often stakeholders will share similar pain points that you can address with comparable or shared solutions. As you learn with and from one stakeholder group, you will then slowly work through your list to see which stakeholder group you need to focus on next. This will eventually help you produce a 360-degree understanding of the systems, interactions, and opportunities connected to your challenge.

So, pause for a few moments here and think: Who are all of the stakeholders internal and external to the challenge, and which group will I/we focus on first?

## Getting Stakeholder-Centered

The final piece of this foundational work of packaging the challenge is to begin the shift from your own and organization-centered thinking to stakeholder-centered thinking. So far, you've thought about what *you* are experiencing as a challenge in your organization, and now it's time to think about and hypothesize how the *stakeholder* you've selected might be impacted by your challenge.

To get more stakeholder-centered, I ask that you write an imaginary hypothesized direct quote from the stakeholder. These quotes can take the form of what people want or a struggle they are facing. This is just an early exercise, so please do not focus on perfection. Let's say your challenge is, "Our city needs more accessible, affordable, high-quality preschool options," and let's say your initial stakeholder group are "caregivers who are on a waiting list for resources." An example quote could be, "I want my child to go to a good preschool so that they do well when they get to elementary school, but I can't afford a high-quality preschool, and I earn too much to qualify for subsidy support."

Hypothesizing at this early stage about how you think stakeholders would talk about the challenge in their own words is not only a helpful exercise to center the stakeholder but also a learning anchor point that you will return to after you interact with stakeholders using empathy interviewing.

So, pause for a few moments here and think: What is your hypothesized stakeholder quote? How do you think the stakeholder would talk about the challenge?

## PAUSE AND CONSIDER

**THIS IS** an exciting first step because you are choosing your starting point and getting clarity! Choosing a challenge on which to focus can be difficult, but it is so important to pick one. Often, organizational leaders will determine the "big challenges" to be tackled, but every person in the sector has something connected to their work that is uncertain and that could use investigation and exploration; the key is to start learning.

What is your challenge? This is usually one sentence about what you want to address and explore. Remember, this is your first draft or hypothesis of your challenge, and you will see how it is shaped by your learning. If you form a team to work on this challenge, your sentence will be further shaped by your team input. So, what is the challenge you want to address?

Now think about this challenge and list *all* of the stakeholders impacted, internally and externally. Look at your list and prioritize one stakeholder group based on their pain, frustration, need, and potential for impact. Be as specific as possible (e.g., are you talking about all parents or are you trying to address the needs of single parents, stepparents, foster parents, teen parents, grandparents caring for grandchildren, etc.)?

- How did completing those three activities feel? Were they helpful? Did they both open and focus your thinking?

- If you are working with a team, do you feel like you have shared alignment and clarity about your challenge, the stakeholder, and the stakeholder's perspective?

- How are these three activities similar to or different from what you typically do in your organization when you notice a challenge?

# Work Together to Address Challenges

A
N INDIVIDUAL can absolutely gain tremendous learning and create significant impact in their work and organization using these skills. If you are a team of one, a lone founder, have a small team, or prefer not to work in a team, you can absolutely still use these skills.

That said, forming and working in teams is very powerful and helpful because, at its most simple benefit, you have more hands on deck contributing energy and attention, as well as a diversity of perspectives, experiences, input, and knowledge.

The very first skill of the PAUSE framework, Package the Challenge, includes two parts. Part one is about getting aligned, having clarity, and sharing information about your challenge and stakeholder, and you begin to shift to a stakeholder perspective. The second part of Package the Challenge is focused on working together to address challenges.

To set the stage for understanding the power and importance of teamwork, there are three provocations that are fundamentally important. They are:

- What if we created value for each other?
- What if we learned together?
- What if we shared power?

## Creating Value for Each Other

As I mentioned, you often hear people talking about creating value in more business-type settings, but we often don't consider or formalize how we create value not only for our external stakeholders but also for one another *inside* our organizations.

While it is paramount to center external stakeholders, such as community members that you exist to support, a high-functioning organization considers how *staff* treat one another, work together to problem-solve, share information, and collaborate. Within organizations there are many stakeholders represented in diverse departments and programs, and at different levels. Staff, leaders, and colleagues deserve value created for them, and just as our external stakeholders won't buy into potential solutions that don't make their lives easier, faster, more pleasurable, and so on, staff won't buy in for the very same reasons.

*We often know very little about what our stakeholders, including our colleagues and community members, find valuable and how they would express their definition of "value."* At the most basic level, it is nearly impossible to create value for someone you don't understand or with whom you don't communicate. Distance and disconnection, which seem to be inevitable parts of large organizations, not only impact the degree to which an organization has a culture of learning and innovation, but will also erode your ability to address your communities' greatest needs.

A conversation I had with a new CEO of an organization has stuck with me and I think illustrates this internal/external connection. He shared that his new leadership style, recent strategic initiatives (which included diversity, equity, and inclusion work), and the ways that he was asking big, bold questions like, "How are we really serving our mission?" were causing pushback from some of his staff. These staff were subverting his authority with nuanced "pokes" or language that questioned his every decision, and these staff were not showing up to do the work with commitment.

Part of what drove the efforts of the new CEO was that he had received feedback from numerous community members and partners (whose feedback previously was not solicited) that what they saw on the website and brochures did not match what they experienced when they interacted with the organization's staff and programs. They could feel and report instances of the disconnect between their experience and the mission, vision, values, and program goals (there are those shadow values and institutional betrayal/failure dynamics popping up). Their negative interactions had eroded trust and created alternative narratives in the community about what the organization was "really about." This example reinforces how often, if there are disconnects internally, they will filter out to reach external stakeholders, partners, and other supporters.

No organization, including its leadership and culture, is perfect, but one of the most powerful ways to think about your role in an organization, whether you are internally or externally connected, is to focus on *value*. And to be clear, when I say value, I mean relationship, reciprocity, and respect, rather than transaction.

So, considering value connected to your internal work and functions of the organization, think about how you would answer these three questions.

- What value do you create for the organization and your colleagues?

- How do you make the work easier, more efficient and effective, more enjoyable, more impactful?

- What value does the organization (and your colleagues) create for you and how does this show up?

It is powerful and transformative to think of our work as a *value exchange.* To be most successful, we really need to create value for each other; it is a two-way street. When mutual value is present, it creates beautiful ripples. Value exchange creates trust, care, kindness, and shared benefit, and the more value you create internally, the more value you will create externally. This value exchange applies not only to community members but also to funders and collaborators, and, really, we should be applying this lens to our personal relationships as well.

High-functioning organizations and relationships that prioritize value exchange also include shared power and honoring the complementary roles that we all play to create social change.

Unfortunately, value exchange is often interrupted and fractured by hierarchies and silos. The barriers we intentionally and unintentionally construct in our organizations often interrupt the flow of exchange. Power asymmetries (a term I first learned from George Aye, cofounder and director of innovation at Greater Good Studio) inequitably value people and resources—for example, "the bosses" versus "frontline staff," or this department or program versus that department or program. By upholding a "this is how *we* do it" stance, work processes and knowledge can become isolated, territorial, and insulated from critique.

When I ask people to think about the value they provide to their team and organization, they often can more easily identify the value breakdowns. Most people can more easily name the person or people they work with who drive them bananas and make their days harder than they need to be than see how they, themselves, add value—or don't. While it may be easier to consider how others cause frustration, it is essential that we all pause to answer the question, "How might *I* be making the work of another person, department, or organization harder, more complicated, frustrating, or even painful?"

We rarely step back and consider how *our* name might be on the tip of someone's tongue or imagine in what ways *we* might be the reason a colleague dreads coming to work. What space in someone's relationship and time off might you occupy when a colleague needs to vent to their partner or friends?

I once worked with a department within a large organization that needed to improve the quality of the services they provided to community members. When they made their list of stakeholders, the list included another department in their organization that was essential to their success. When it was time for the team to dive more deeply into understanding this stakeholder group, the team was super reluctant to talk to them because there was a history of conflict and deep frustration between the staff of the two departments. One team member decided that she would cross over to "the other side" and asked, "How does my department make your work harder?" and "In what ways could we make your work easier?"

The staff in the other department were stunned that someone from her group would make this vulnerable connection, and they very graciously and honestly shared what they needed. It turned out that their frustrations made sense; the two departments shared many of the same goals, and staff had very similar ideas about how to improve community members' experiences. This one person having a few honest chats opened new pathways for communication and collaboration that had been at a stalemate for years.

Sometimes distance and separation are not as dramatic as outright conflict. You and your colleagues might be so focused on the execution of your mission that you don't build in time for connection, empathy, curiosity, and shared learning. This is one of the reasons I love forming and working with teams that break across silos and expand through hierarchies to address challenges. Creating value is about listening, seeing value in diverse perspectives, and codesigning solutions that change people's daily lives, internally and externally.

Above, I mention the term "silos" and I talk about this a few times, so let me share my definition here. Silos are found in communities and organizations when agencies, departments, or teams become separate, often impacting their willingness and ability to share learning and collaborate. It also can result in hyperconcentrated skills, responsibilities, and resources in pockets across the organization, which create further isolation and feelings of "our work" versus "your/ their work." When a community ecosystem and organization does not have strategies to prevent and/or connect silos, impact and culture can suffer.

## Learning Together

Just as I said that in the worst cases information in organizations is guarded and weaponized, the lack of sharing information and learning is usually unintentional. *Most organizations have not even thought about or set up a process by which they share and record institutional learning and memory.* I think the cause is mostly our obsession with heads-down action and execution; we do not pause and place value on learning as a metric of our success.

In our "go, go, go" culture and the urgency we all feel working in social change, we rarely pause to consider how our siloed and disconnected work creates tremendous waste. I have seen, in multiple organizations, diverse departments working on the same challenge without ever talking to each other. I've also seen multiple times where one person has all of the knowledge about how to do something, or all the background of an important relationship or initiative, and they never cross-train or share. It is foolish, risky, and a touch infuriating. It makes logical sense that people share what they're trying, what they're learning, and how they work, but they don't share because they are often hoarding power, they are "too busy," or there is no mechanism for sharing in place.

## Sharing Power

Think about the last time your organization formed a committee or pursued a large initiative. Who got invited to that proverbial "table"? When you last noticed that one of your projects or programs wasn't hitting its desired metrics, who was engaged in a conversation to brainstorm about what might be an explanation or a potential way to shift those outcomes? What I have seen is that most organizations will engage the thoughts and feedback of those who hold the most institutional power, including executive leadership teams, directors, managers, and board members.

This reinforces how we often do not center stakeholders and those who are closest to the problem, pain, and possibilities. I cannot tell you the number of frontline staff members who have never had anyone know who they are, what they do, and the perspectives that *they* can contribute to the work. It's almost as if leaders believe that professional investment should be provided only to a certain level or tenure of staff member, but I have met unacknowledged staff who have large documents on their computers full of program and process improvement ideas that they've never shared with anyone because "no one's ever asked." It is critical that everyone have the ability to provide feedback, so that not only are you tapping the superpowers and insights of all staff, but also your work is rooted in sharing information and learning, and centered in equitable access to power.

## Teamwork in Collaborative Partnerships Is Key

All I have shared about being informed and aligned, and creating value and sharing power, apply on overdrive when you work in collaborative partnerships. Can you imagine how your work with collaborative partners would shift if you considered how you create value for each other (or not), how you share learning and information, and how you share equitable access to power and decision-making?

I've stopped being shocked when I'm asked to support existing collaborative projects and representatives from partner agencies show up, many of whom have coexisted for months or years, and they still do not know each other's names, what they do in their organizations, and about their organizations' diverse and complementary missions. Some are even still fuzzy on why they are there and the point of the collaboration.

It is imperative that you consider these aspects of value, learning, and power to better root your collective work so that everyone feels connected to one another and to the tasks at hand. Years ago, in a fit of frustration after seeing yet another disconnected coalition, I drafted these twenty questions that collaborative partners should consider and ask one another *before* they begin their work together.

1 Why are we here? What is the challenge we are here to address?

2 What is the vision and what are the intended outcomes?

3 Why was my organization asked to be here?

4 How have our separate organizations addressed this challenge in the past? What worked and what didn't?

5 What work have we done together in the past? What was positive and negative about that experience?

6 How was I selected to represent my organization?

7 What are you looking for me and for each person to provide?

8 How much time do you estimate my organization and I will have to dedicate to this project?

9 What are the financial resources for this project? What are the total dollar amounts?

10 How will money be distributed and how will these funds be divided among the partners?

11 How will my organization be recognized for our contributions to the program or project?

12 Will my organization be able to present our own individual data and experiences to funders directly?

13 How will my agency provide feedback about the success of the collaboration and the functionality of our partnership?

14 Outside of this project, what are the key priority areas that your agency is focused on?

15 What are some of the most significant challenges and opportunities you are currently tackling as an organization?

16  What are some elements about this collaboration that make you the most nervous or that you are the most concerned about in terms of impacting the success?

17  What have you experienced in the past with other agencies that has generated successful collaborative work?

18  What have you experienced in the past that did not work well for collaboration and led to disappointing results?

19  What must be true for this to be a successful collaboration? In other words, what assumptions might we be making about our work together that could make or break our ability to reach our vision of success?

20  What are some ground rules that are very important to your organization and us working together?

These provocations are hardly ever asked but are key to avoiding the subtle (or not so subtle), competitive, and passive-aggressive dynamics that can crop up between multiple organizations working on the same initiative. I have seen the breakdown in impact especially when a collaboration was initiated (or required) by a funder or other outside entity, or led by a powerful convener in the community that relied on "trickle-down impact." This usually looks like a convening organization being granted most of the funding and power and distributing smaller bits of resources to partner agencies, assuming and expecting that the collective impact will be elevated by their shared commitment.

This arrangement can be tricky and is most successful when significant and shared transparency, respect, trust, and communication are present (along with equitable distribution of financial resources). By creating value (and shared definitions of what value means to each entity), forging mechanisms and pathways for sharing learning and information, and providing equitable access to power and funding, these investments and partnerships can be much better positioned to achieve their collective goals. If all the collaborative partners have a shared language, process, and skills, they can create even greater impact. I have seen this magic develop in many collaborative initiatives when all partners used the PAUSE skills to tackle a challenge in unity.

## Learning as a Team Is Powerful

While you absolutely can make change as just one person, I love teamwork because not only is a diverse group of lovely humans making huge progress learning about challenges, stakeholders, and potential solutions, but also they are learning a tremendous amount about themselves and each other on the journey.

I love seeing the individual shifts, the team dynamics emerge and transform, and the deep level of connection people feel to each other, the challenge, and their stakeholders. Even though it is, of course, less desirable, I still love the inevitable conflict, learning struggles, and obstacles that team dynamics can create. Both the positive and negative aspects of working in teams are normal, healthy, and generative. The connection of perspectives, expertise, and ideas is so powerful and truly drives learning in new ways.

### Key Team Considerations

Teams are key to shared learning, and they are especially powerful when they use common practices, skills, and language. Often, just having the scaffolding of support to pause can produce results beyond your expectations.

*Teams of three to five people are the most efficient in getting work done.* This is pretty different from how most of us work. How many times have you been asked to work on a twenty-plus-person task force or tried to make progress in a room of twelve individuals? The larger the team, the slower and potentially more difficult your work will be because you need more time to include every person's perspective on moving the project forward.

Your goal is to form a small and diverse team that breaks across hierarchies and silos. This team will learn together to tackle your challenge. You may be concerned about the people not on the team, but usually these additional individuals are deeply engaged in other key roles, such as being interviewed about the challenge, being included in a solution test, assisting with research, or attending presentations about your learning, and they do not need to be on the core team. If you are chuckling to yourself at this point because your organization equals three people total, then all three of you can work as a team, and you can also invite others such as volunteers, board members, community members that you support with your programs, or partners.

There are several key considerations when putting together a team.

**Who needs to be a part of addressing this challenge?** Who is connected to or has experience/expertise related to this challenge? Who will be involved in implementing a potential solution?

It makes sense to include people who know something about the challenge, and who will be connected to following the evidence to its decision-making ends. Be thoughtful when considering all layers of connection. For example, to improve the employee onboarding process, a team could include newly hired *and* longer-term employees in frontline *and* manager-level positions, as well as representatives from HR.

A cautionary note: Sometimes people who are less helpful are added to a team. Often, a leader will want to include people who may not be directly connected to a challenge because they want to "expose" them to the framework or provide professional development. Unfortunately, if someone is not connected to the challenge and to its potential implementation, it can feel odd to everyone involved and potentially disrupt the learning process.

You might be asking, "What about including stakeholders on your team?" Yes, you absolutely can and should include stakeholders on a team, and in my experience, how the team is comprised depends on the challenge.

For example, some challenges are mostly internal-facing, and the team is comprised of staff who touch that challenge, so in some ways the work is 100 percent stakeholder-led. Other challenges have teams composed of half staff, half community members, as both are deeply impacted by the challenge. From what I've experienced, some projects would have been impossible to support if we did not have community stakeholders on the team, as they opened doors to include others in the community. It truly depends on, and is up to, the team to consider all the ways that stakeholders can be included.

If you want to root your work in equity and shared power, please do not overlook what has at times become accepted and commonplace in the sector. All individuals on a team should be compensated for their time, feedback, and amazing contributions. For example, for a multimillion-dollar project funded by a federal agency that provided no money for community compensation, a condition of my work was that I be able to fundraise to ensure community members got paid. I raised $100,000; half of the funds were used in the form of gift cards to pay people directly for their participation and also included stipends to compensate people for their time spent coordinating events, organizing activities, and connecting with community members. The other half provided funding for projects that community members wanted to design and lead. It was fantastic how this respect and compensation brought community partners and members to life—few organizations are ever granted funds outside of convoluted grant processes that are unrestricted and provided with trust.

**Who has experience working with the stakeholder group?** It is very important to include people who are already deeply connected to the stakeholder on whom you are focusing. This is where shared power is very important, since the people least often invited for professional development are usually those most closely connected to your external stakeholders. If you are focused on an internal challenge, include stakeholder representation from all areas touched by the challenge. For example, a team that was addressing a challenge in grants management included representatives from fund development, programs, evaluation, finance, and legal.

**Who are your early adopters for working differently?** These are your "troublemakers," who love to ask questions and challenge the status quo. You can usually count on them to bring original insights. They often ask, "Why do we do it this way?" "What might be possible if…?" "I just read this cool case study and maybe we should try ＿＿＿＿＿ too!" Sometimes these staff take the form of the newest person in your organization, or at times are seen as "troublemaking" due to their younger age. When I get to work with these team members, I am thrilled, not just because of my bias toward troublemaking, but also because I love the inquiry, curiosity, and creativity they can bring.

**Who are your potential skeptics or resisters?** These are
the people who need to see or experience the framework in
action and are often staff who enjoy the status quo and "the
way we've always done it." They usually are seen as the negative person who stands in the way of progress and tend to say
things like, "If it ain't broke, don't fix it," "We tried that before
and it didn't work," and "That's just not possible." Sometimes,
these are staff members who have worked in your organization for a longer time and are possibly seen as "stodgier" due
to their older age. I am thrilled when I get to work with these
team members because they hold institutional memory, their
personal identities are connected to their work, and they have
deep relationships.

It can also be helpful to have resisters on the team to ensure
that they see the process inside and out so they can experience
its power, which will hopefully reduce or remove the likeli-
hood that they will stand in the way of others' learning.

**Who will be able to dedicate time to address this challenge?**
People often worry about the time that using new skills can
take. After the initial training, most of the individuals and
teams I support dedicate about two to four hours a week to do
research, conduct interviews, test solutions, and hold team or
shared learning meetings. I totally get that most people still
have day-to-day work they need to complete, so this work is a
bit extra and requires a shift of time.

If you are working in a team, of course, you want all team
members to show up 100 percent. As we know, life and the
unexpected happen, so it is very helpful to have a team of all
dedicated members so they can fully share the responsibility
of moving the work forward.

I often hear from teams that they rarely get dedicated time
to pause and focus on a challenge, and that they get more work
done in this condensed time than they usually do in months

and even years. Also, most individuals who use the PAUSE skills for one challenge see opportunities to work differently to address other challenges and use the skills into the future.

In later chapters, I will briefly talk about how to apply the PAUSE skills to teamwork, and on my book website, NoMore StatusQuoBook.com, I have multiple, very specific articles about my lessons learned working with many, many teams over the past ten-plus years. These articles include ways to ground the team and strategies to unlock the power of diverse team positionalities, team dynamics, team roles, and more. They provide valuable insights, so please check them out.

## PAUSE AND CONSIDER

**THERE ARE** so many layers and nuances to how humans work together, and these nuances can be both the beauty and the beast of this work. We are each so complex and tension-filled; we are each skilled and visionary in our own ways, and we are each also total stinkers and super difficult in our own ways. Melding together a set of diverse humans who shift day to day, even hour by hour, can be really hard. But I'm convinced it's also where the magic lies.

To truly see each other, understand each other, listen, share power, and cocreate to address social problems, we must pause to ask different questions and behave in different ways. It feels so good when people create value for us, and we owe it to our colleagues and stakeholders to think about how we create value for them. Consider these questions:

- First, think of a person in your organization, department, division, wherever you work, who makes your life easier. How do you feel when you interact with them? How would you describe them to another person?

- Now consider how *you* create value for another person in your organization, department, or division. How do you make their life easier? How do you think they feel when they interact with you? How do you think they would describe you to another person?

- Now ponder the reverse. Think of a person in your organization, department, or division who makes your life harder. How do you feel when you interact with them? How would you describe them to another person?

- Now consider how *you* might make life harder for another person in your organization, department, or division. How do you make their life more difficult? How do you think the person feels when they interact with you? How do you think they would describe you to another person?

- Think about how information in your organization is collected, stored, shared, and requested.

  - Do you have mechanisms that support organizational learning?

  - How is information and learning shared over time, accounting for staff changes?

  - Are there areas where information and learning get stuck?

- Are there people in the organization who would benefit from having all or more of the information they need to do their work?

- Are there ways in which you might build in time and space to learn together?

- Think about how power is shared in your organization.

  - Who gets to provide input and feedback?

  - How are decisions made about which solutions to pursue?

  - How are a variety of stakeholders included and represented?

  - For training or learning support, who gets access to opportunities and organizational resources?

- Think about your collaborative partnerships.

  - Do you know what everyone's definition of value is?

  - Do your collaborative partners feel aligned and informed?

  - Are there key questions you might need to ask to deepen your shared understanding of the challenge and your roles?

  - Do you have ways to share learning and power?

While the nuances of teams are addressed in several articles on my book website, NoMoreStatusQuoBook.com, I want to offer these additional provocations.

- How often do you and people in your organization work in teams? What works well with your current teamwork and what could use some improvement?

- How often do people in your organization work in teams that cross hierarchical levels, silos, different departments, or divisions?

- Think of the last team you were on. How was the team formed? In what ways did each of you connect to or represent a skill or perspective related to the challenge and/or stakeholder?

- Have you ever experienced both "troublemakers" and "resisters" on your team? Which most feels like you and why?

- When a team is formed, how is the team oriented to the work? Do they know what they are there to work on and why? Do they know why they were chosen?

- Think of *your* challenge and stakeholder. Start to imagine whom you might want to have on a team and what value they each bring.

# 8

# Assess Uncertainty

YOU'VE COMPLETED the first PAUSE skill, Package the Challenge. You've identified what challenge you want to address; you've selected the stakeholder group to focus on first; and, if possible and desired, you have formed a team and aligned the team to begin work together.

The next PAUSE skill you can pull out of your toolbox when you are facing uncertainty is all about running *toward* uncertainty, rather than running away from the unknown. What I have learned in this work is that you really have to sit in the uncertainty and take time to call it out, name it, share it, prioritize it, and address it.

None of us is immune to the icky feelings that come with uncertainty, and as we've discussed, our bodies *really* don't like it. We are not alone in feeling increasingly uncertain as a species, as a sector, and as individuals. What we are learning more than ever is that *the shifting of our reality and the uncertainty that results are our reality. We have been and will ever be shifting, transforming, and redefining.* That may make us feel destabilized, but these shifts also provide opportunities for much needed advancement and evolution. It is time for us as individuals and as a sector to embrace this moment and use new skills to navigate our unavoidably changing world.

Our typical way of working is creating those "giant triangles of waste" by assuming we have what we need to create a successful program, service, or process. But often, when we really think about it, we are not working on projects that are highly known—there is uncertainty and a lot that we don't know.

We've set up structures in our organizations that are designed around "knowing things." Leaders (think of your executive team, middle management, board of directors) are expected to know about strategic planning and decision-making, be visionary and skilled at connecting the dots, excel at leading others, and have past experiences that have positioned them to do well in their current roles. Pause here and consider leaders with whom you have worked who fit this description, along with the many who do not. There are many books about leadership and how to improve those qualities, but one thing that is true for leaders is that they are not supposed to be "wrong" or uncertain.

Can you imagine a boss who, whenever they were asked to provide clarity or make a decision, always said, "I don't know"? We expect that our leaders will know the answers and have a plan. Their behavior reinforces this expectation, as they rarely publicly express uncertainty and usually have an idea or recommendation for how to forge ahead.

But while this is typical and expected, I would argue that saying "I don't know" is one the best things any of us can say, and it is one of the ultimate expressions of vulnerability, especially for leaders.

Vulnerability, open communication, and shared power are essential for authentic trust—and relationship building (and perhaps even organizational success and impact)—and adopting these principals is one of the very best ways for leaders to show that they support new ways of working.

I also must point out that while vulnerability is key, it is not always accessible, safe, or comfortable for all. Many in the social impact space, especially colleagues of color, staff who are LGBTQ2+, those who are disabled, and many others, for many reasons, may not be able to show up vulnerably (or even as their full selves), and must code-switch to appease expectations and avoid consequences.

While this a daily reality that must be addressed with deep personal and organizational culture work, there are alternative ways in which all leaders can set the tone when uncertainty arises. Instead of saying, "Here's my idea. Let's get to work," it is so much more generative and powerful to say, "I don't know; this challenge, stakeholder, and potential solution seem pretty uncertain. Let's apply some new skills to learn together." This openness to possibility is even more important, as the concentration of power in leaders is often distant from the power and perspectives of staff and community members.

It is key to act and lead with a beginner's mind, rather than an expert's mind. Consider Shunryu Suzuki's words: "In the beginner's mind there are many possibilities, but in the expert's there are few." This is especially true when you or someone on your team is a subject matter expert; when you have extensive backgrounds of knowledge, it can often be difficult to integrate both new and conflicting information. When you lead with an expert's mind, it shapes your expectations of what will happen and what you think will work. The good news is that even if you're an expert, you still do not have, and do not have to have, all the answers all the time. You can commit to centering stakeholder priorities and apply your skills to their best and highest use. You are not asking stakeholders how to do your job, but working together to make sure that what you codesign will be the most successful and impactful. When we adopt a "beginner's mind," there are unlimited possibilities for learning and outcomes.

There are three guiding questions for the second skill of the PAUSE framework, Assess Uncertainty:

- What if we identified what was uncertain?

- What if we assumed we were wrong?

- What if success was saving time, money, and energy by not building solutions?

So, what if we identified what was uncertain? How often does that happen, that someone asks you what you don't know? How often do you ask yourself that? I know that before I started using and teaching these new skills, I had *a lot* of answers, most of which I thought were pretty good. My past coworkers (including leaders) and I never pondered the unknown or held space to talk about what we didn't know and needed to learn about the challenge at hand or our stakeholders. We just went into planning mode and started creating what we thought would make a positive impact. We never once considered that by just plowing ahead we might create waste or harm.

I once was told a story that illustrates this potential harm. There was a director, "Jamie," whose organization had just launched a new community-wide initiative to address a huge social problem, and it was their job to uncover how the program should proceed. The CEO of the organization, "Pat," was sharing the initiative's vision for how it would change lives with funders and powerful community partners in order to gain buy-in and financial support. Meanwhile, Jamie was learning a lot, uncovering and untangling not only the intertwined and broken systems connected to the initiative but also the weak community collaboration and competition that had kept the status quo sticky and deeply rooted. Jamie came to realize that they had really no idea how the organization was going to address the depth, breadth, and complexity of change that would be required in order to benefit community members. While CEO Pat was shaking hands, making promises, and collecting big gifts, Jamie, the program director, developed panic attacks due to extreme stress and anxiety and was considering leaving the organization.

## Knowing What You Don't Know

Sometimes, harm is created by oversights fueled by our ignorance. For context here, I want to share a story my grandmother used to tell me. When I was upset about not knowing an answer and said things like, "Ugh, I'm dumb," she would share how she felt many times after immigrating to the United States. She said that when she felt stupid and frustrated by all that she did not know, my grandfather would say to her, "You are not stupid, you are just ignorant." My immediate response was that Grandpa was not nice to call her that, but she would go on to say, "He said, 'You are ignorant,' and all that means is that you just haven't learned it ... *yet*." Reframing how she felt helped her be patient and know that she would continue to accumulate new information and knowledge, and this has always stuck with me too.

So really, we are all ignorant about so many different things. While some of our knowledge gaps might include a lack of understanding of particle physics or how to speak a love language, we also have large gaps in essential knowledge, like why we do our work the way we do, how decisions are made, and the greatest needs of our coworkers and community stakeholders. These gaps influence the impact we make every day across the sector.

**ALL POSSIBLE KNOWLEDGE**

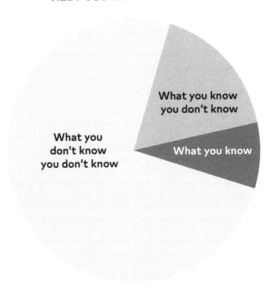

Looking at the pie chart, you can see that the full circle is all possible knowledge and it has three main components, what we know, what we know we don't know, and the largest section, representing the items that will pop up later because we don't even know we're missing that knowledge. I often jokingly ask at this stage of learning, "Do you want the hot mess now or later?" *You will hit that moment you did not expect and it will potentially derail your plan, so do you want to expose all that you need to learn now or wait until later, when your investment and commitment are deep?*

Let me share one of my personal examples of when I unintentionally created a ton of waste with the best of intentions. I worked at an organization that was focused on preventing skin cancer. We noticed in our very hot climate that parents were unintentionally exposing their young children to high amounts of intense sun and UV exposure, the cause of preventable but disfiguring and deadly skin cancers. We saw babies in strollers without sun covers and children with no hats, so we decided to create an educational program that would focus on new parents to teach them about sun safety. Our intent was that parents would learn all the ways to protect the fragile skin of their young children, from the earliest start of life, and prevent future skin cancer.

We partnered with a manufacturer of sun hats for babies; they gave us a wonderful deal on the hats, which we imprinted with our logo. We created a very detailed brochure with all the basic information that parents would need. The brochure was translated and back-translated in English and Spanish, and we included culturally diverse images from multiple photography sessions to make sure the images represented all of our community members. We partnered with a local hospital maternity unit that agreed to distribute these adorable baby sun safety informational bags to all new families. We wrote a grant to a national foundation and were awarded financial support for the project, and we secured an individual donor who also made the project launch possible. We even applied to a competition that was focused on how to write a strong case for support, and we won! We were riding high after months of extensive work.

The project launched and we expected to get feedback from the families who received these gift bags. In each bag, we had included a postcard that asked parents to answer a few brief survey questions. We waited and waited and received a small handful of the postcards back. We contacted our hospital partners and they said they had distributed hundreds of bags. We started to wonder if we should renew orders of the items in order to create additional bags. Over time, and after a continued lack of feedback, the project fizzled out, and I, who had spearheaded the project, left the organization to pursue new opportunities.

It wasn't until I left the organization and was exposed to these new ways of working that it became crystal clear why the program failed. *We never talked to a single expectant or new parent when we were designing the program.* We also never talked to hospital staff about how they interacted with new parents in their daily work. And even though almost all of us in that organization had had our own children, we somehow totally forgot what those early days in the hospital were like after having a baby. We completely missed that new parents are essentially walking zombies juggling bliss, pain, absolute exhaustion, and a lot of fear about being sent home with their little vulnerable and beautiful human.

We also totally forgot about all the information and stimulus parents experience after giving birth. Not only do you watch required videos, encounter experts on feeding, and entertain family and visitors, but you are given bags and bags of free formula, diaper kits, and instruction guides. It became so evident to me that we interacted with parents at the absolute worst possible time to try to make sure that they "understood sun safety was their number one priority." It makes me laugh when I think of the absurdity of our bag arriving at that moment. I swear that our project made perfect sense at the time, not only to us but also to so many others, and it was a complete failure. Yes, some families got a cute hat and a brochure that maybe they unpacked and reviewed at some point, but in no way did our impact match our intent, and in no way did we significantly improve the sun protection or skin cancer prevention of young children in our community.

This is just one story of how, by not pausing to consider what we knew and didn't know about our challenge and stakeholders, we created a tremendous waste of time, supplies, donated money, and new relationships. The other interesting thing this story illustrates is that we carry gaps in our knowledge even if we have shared experiences with the stake-holder. On the baby sun hat team, every person had given birth to a child, adopted a young child, or was also a grand-parent, and none of us ever saw that distributing the bags in the maternity ward might be problematic.

I've seen knowledge gaps pop up in other challenges and even in some of the most connected, grassroots-led, social justice-minded organizations. These teams said they "knew" their community, these were "their people," and yet the solu-tions they explored were actually pretty weak and at times potentially harmful; some were even in direct conflict with what they heard from stakeholders. It is important for all of us to be open to exploring and uncovering uncertainty so that we listen and codesign with humility to create amazing impact. This counts for work in collaborative partnerships as well, so identifying your collective uncertainties is very powerful to guide your roadmap for learning.

The next provocation of this Assess Uncertainty skill is, What if we assumed we were wrong? This is another ques-tion we rarely ask of ourselves and the sector. We usually just build with the assumptions that we are onto something and we can pull it off. What if your understanding of the stake-holder has some gaps that are created by your own perspective and limited experience? What if there are other solutions and challenges that you're not even aware of that could be really important to consider?

Assuming you're wrong doesn't have to be depressing or absolutely exhausting. Asking questions about what you don't know or what might be missing can actually become exhil-arating and empowering because these questions give you a blueprint for how to focus your work. Even though you may think you're inviting uncertainty and discomfort when you directly consider these questions, you are actually achieving the desired outcome—that release of dopamine in your brain—because you are focused on how to move forward. You are making progress, making decisions about your next steps, and crafting a plan for how you will get that information, and that is exciting. You are rejecting the status quo jump to execution and you are committing to learning how best to create a positive impact.

The last provocation of Assess Uncertainty is, What if success was saving time, money, and energy by not building solutions? The idea of saving time and money sounds good, but in the sector, we are in no way rewarded for *not building* things. We get grant funding and donations by creating and delivering programs; we get board and executive support by creating and delivering programs; and the community knows us for creating and delivering programs. I think you get the idea. Rarely, if ever, do we talk about what we haven't created or what we created and delivered that totally flopped. Organizations must keep up the external facade of smooth and deliberate vision and operation, and we must project to all stakeholders that we've got it right and know how to create impact.

As in the example of the hoarding challenge, even teams that learn quickly that a potential solution is not viable become excited after their initial feelings of disappointment. They are able to acknowledge and recognize how learning that something wouldn't work in four hours versus four months or four years feels so much better! It's invigorating to think, "What else can I consider, question, or test to prove or disprove, and quickly share with others?"

People who embrace the PAUSE skills and integrate these learning superpowers often become rock stars in their organizations because they're able to move through learning efficiently and effectively. *We have to take the "F word"—Failure—off the table and reward and celebrate the moments when we learn something we should not do, when we decide not to pursue an idea, and when we pause in the busyness of the work to identify areas of uncertainty.* This also works for projects that get really fast and early confirmation, or that find a solution no one even had on their radar. So, by identifying uncertainty and applying new skills, not only can you ignore ideas that deserve to be pushed to the wayside, but you can also elevate and accelerate potential ideas that have early validation.

## We Work This Way Because We're Biased

One of my favorite thinkers, Michael O'Bryan from Humanature (humanature.works), was the first person to make me think about how by what we design, we are imagining the future for other people. Since we've established that we are all designers in this work (yes, even if we don't hold that title), it is essential that we acknowledge that our viewpoints, experiences, and ideas are limited by our own positionalities, and that we are biased. In case you are under the illusion that you are not biased, John Manoogian III took the time to categorize all 188 different forms of cognitive biases and organize them into an open-source Cognitive Bias Codex. I recommend you check it out and see which of the forms of biases you can relate to.

We need to accept as fact that we all are biased. As Kerry Edelstein, founder of Research Narrative states, "Humans are simply fallible to unconscious bias. We don't mean to be biased; we don't want to be biased. But we are. And we only get past it by pointing it out to one another." Identifying and addressing our biases is challenging because we look for information that matches or affirms them.

The Ladder of Inference shows how our brains process and calcify information. As you see in the illustration, at the very bottom of the ladder (the first rung or starting point), you observe data. From there, you very rapidly select the data you desire, add meaning to that data, make assumptions and interpretations based on your beliefs, draw conclusions and generalizations, and then adopt beliefs that drive your actions. What's super tricky is that once you've adopted beliefs upon which you take action, you select data that reinforces your beliefs, so you start to create this loop of just selecting data that reinforces your perspectives. This process visually includes many steps, but your brain snaps through these thoughts and actions in seconds.

What happens in just seconds, often unnoticed, unfortunately impacts our work and the future we imagine for others.

Here is a powerful example that illustrates the role of bias. One day I had the opportunity to sit on a hiring panel of one of my clients as they interviewed candidates. In the candidate pool were two individuals who had both worked for the division that was connected to Section 8 housing. The first interviewee (I'll call him Charlie) shared that his job was to inspect the homes once residents had moved out to ensure that the lights, heating and cooling, water, and so on were all operational for the next resident. While he described his work, he said flippantly, "These are not places where any of *us* would want to live" and that the quality of the home didn't really matter because "most of the people who live there are crazy."

Later in the day, we interviewed the other individual, "Monica," whose job was to work one-on-one with people who were applying for Section 8 housing and were being placed on a very long waiting list. She described to us how much paperwork and perseverance it takes for people to not only get on the list but also move through the process when their number does come up for housing. Monica expressed admiration and respect for these individuals because she saw all that they

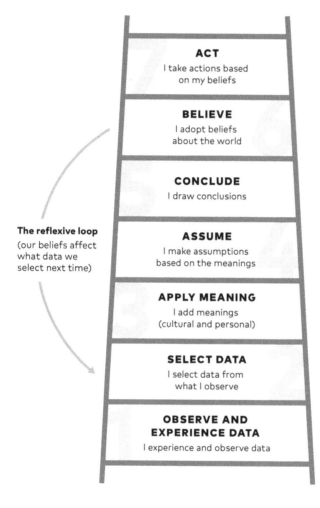

THE LADDER OF INFERENCE

**ACT**
I take actions based
on my beliefs

**BELIEVE**
I adopt beliefs
about the world

**CONCLUDE**
I draw conclusions

**ASSUME**
I make assumptions
based on the meanings

**APPLY MEANING**
I add meanings
(cultural and personal)

**SELECT DATA**
I select data from
what I observe

**OBSERVE AND
EXPERIENCE DATA**
I experience and observe data

**The reflexive loop**
(our beliefs affect
what data we
select next time)

were juggling and the stress and anxiety that was caused by unstable and scarce housing provided by the city.

It was so amazing to experience the juxtaposition of these two very divergent perspectives just hours apart, and I can say with certainty that their perspectives and empathic connection (or lack thereof) absolutely impacted how they showed up at work and how they took action to support community members. It feels odd to have to state this fact, but if we bring our brains to work, we bring our biases to work.

No one enjoys having their beliefs, which have been reinforced by all of their own personal experiences, challenged. It can feel like a threat or rejection. Especially when in our fast-moving world we're just trying to easily put information in the right mental file folder to keep moving forward with life. This high-speed world doesn't make room for critical thinking, recognizing and holding tension, and making space for times when we realize that four things can be true at once.

The good news is that just as we all can get savvier at navigating uncertainty, we all can also get much better at acknowledging our biases and being wrong. Being wrong *together* is even better. When you work in teams, you are not alone in the discomfort, and you can actually benefit from understanding the diversity of biases and thought loops of others.

## Calling Out Uncertainty

The first thing we do to Assess Uncertainty is pause and sit *in* the uncertainty. By asking different questions, you can identify what you need to learn and prioritize how you will get to that learning; instead of being a barrier, the uncertainty eventually transforms into the engine that drives your work.

In order to uncover your areas of uncertainty, you (and your team, if applicable) need to complete a very simple and generative activity called "What do I know for sure and what do I still need to learn?"

The "what do I know for sure?" question allows you to document what you know to be true, what you have already learned, and what you have data and research to support. Since learning is ever evolving, think of this as a list of hypotheses for what you think you know, and please acknowledge that what you believe, what you think is true, and what you know all might be challenged as you engage with stakeholders and test solutions.

For the "what do I still need to learn?" question, you want to document what you're curious about, questions you have, and any data or information you're lacking.

For the different activities in this book, you will see simple tables and two-by-two graphs that can be easily created and used in any setting. Early in my own learning journey in coaching organizations, I saw how bulky, fancy, printed tools actually limited learning and progress. Individuals would say, "I can't move forward because the tool is in so-and-so's office," or "I don't have it in front of me," or "It's too expensive to print." When I work with teams now, I just have them grab a large sheet of flip chart paper, or even just use wall space, a cube of sticky notes, and a pen or Sharpie, and they get to work. There are also a large number of online collaboration tools that you also can use to create, complete, and track your learning from these different activities individually and as a team.

For this activity, you are thinking of what you know for sure (knowns) and what you still need to learn (unknowns) for both your challenge and the stakeholder.

|  | **Knowns**<br>What do I know for sure? | **Unknowns**<br>What do I still need to learn? |
|---|---|---|
| **Challenge** |  |  |
| **Stakeholder** |  |  |

First, think about your challenge and consider the following prompts or questions to help you brainstorm what you know for sure and what you still need to learn.

Some prompts to stimulate your thinking include:

- What do I know about this challenge from my organization's perspective?

- How do I know this is a challenge?

- What symptoms am I seeing?

- What is the background of this challenge?

- What has my organization tried so far to address this challenge?

- What is working and what's not?

For some of these prompts, you will have answers, and for others, they will raise uncertainty and questions. For example, if you think through any of these question prompts and you say to yourself, "Hmm, I don't know," then write down what it is you're unsure about and place it with the unknowns.

The purpose of this activity is to identify and categorize your knowns and unknowns. This is just a starting point and an activity to ground your thinking and next steps; most of these thoughts will probably shift in some way as you progress in your learning journey.

Once you have identified all of the different knowns and unknowns related to the challenge, then consider what you know for sure and what you still need to learn related to the stakeholder. Think about:

- What does the stakeholder want (what outcomes are they hoping for)?

- What might be some obstacles or barriers standing in their way?

- How is the stakeholder currently trying to address their own problem(s)? What about their current attempts are working or not?

The following example is based on a project with a client, and I will refer to it throughout the remainder of the book as well. There was a team that wanted to explore ways they could increase the recruitment and retention of caregivers in their early childhood home visitation program. They recognized two issues: caregivers in their program were dropping out, and their typical outreach strategies were not leading to new caregiver enrollment. As a note, the team chose to keep "caregivers" broadly defined, as they had many different types of caregivers in their program and recognized that this was an additional initial hypothesis.

Their table looked something like this:

|  | **Knowns**<br>What do I know for sure? | **Unknowns**<br>What do I still need to learn? |
| --- | --- | --- |
| **Challenge** | Enrollment is dropping and we are losing funding.<br><br>We sit at a table for 3 hours to recruit new caregivers and we collect only 3 names.<br><br>We are competing with other tables at public events.<br><br>At other events, like library storytime, we are reaching those caregivers who are already engaged.<br><br>Emails and website are not very helpful. | What else can we do to reach caregivers?<br><br>How much flexibility do we have to try new outreach strategies?<br><br>Who on the staff can do the outreach?<br><br>Where are the best places to reach caregivers? |
| **Stakeholder** | Caregivers are busy.<br><br>Caregivers are stressed.<br><br>Caregivers want the best for their children. | Where are caregivers going for early childhood caregiving support?<br><br>What do caregivers need and want?<br><br>Do those needs vary based on type of caregiver?<br><br>What are caregivers' greatest priorities?<br><br>What barriers are there for caregivers participating in services? |

After you fill out your table with knowns and unknowns, it is time to focus more deeply on your *unknowns* for both your challenge and stakeholder so you can consider which specific areas of uncertainty might be the most important. Look at those two categories on the right side as a whole (unknowns for both your challenge and the stakeholder) and decide which unknowns are the most critical to making progress on addressing your challenge. Place a star or some other indicator on your most important unknowns so you can be ready for the next step of the framework. In this example, it seems pretty important to first begin with an understanding of what caregivers want and need, as well as what gets in their way.

You want to focus on the most important unknowns because this will keep your work focused on what you need to learn first, since you can't address every area of uncertainty at the same time. Getting specific does not mean that you ignore or "lose" the abundance of documentation of all your areas of uncertainty. You may later look at all of the knowns as you proceed on your learning journey and see that some of what you thought was true is now debunked or validated; you may look at your unknowns and see how after some early learning, some unknowns that might have been previously unclear are now better understood, and you might have new unknowns that have been generated by your new learning.

Documentation is key. You have already documented your challenge, stakeholder, and hypothesized quote for how stakeholders might talk about the challenge in their own words. Writing down your knowns and unknowns is the next step of your learning journey. You are tracking and recording, not only to organize your thinking and next steps but also to share with others, especially decision-makers.

**What This Activity Looks like with Your Team**

As I have mentioned, you do not have to have a team to use and benefit from the PAUSE skills, but I want to make sure you feel confident that you can complete these tasks on your own *and* with a team.

The team brainstorms knowns and unknowns individually and adds them to physical or virtual sticky notes. Each person shares their notes, and duplicates and similar ideas are grouped. "Sharing out" looks like a very quick readthrough of each sticky note and not a lengthy explanation of why that sticky note is super important or relevant; this is essential for moving quickly and making sure that everyone is heard. Once everyone has shared, the entire team should discuss which unknowns for both the challenge and stakeholder to prioritize. Place a star or some other indicator on your most important "unknown" sticky notes so that you can be ready for the next step of the framework.

This activity is powerful because you are taking time to learn from and with your team members and to see the variation of thinking they contribute. You might guess that someone who has been with your organization for many years can be helpful in answering the question of what the organization has tried so far and will likely know more about the background of a challenge, while a newer employee might bring a fresh perspective to where symptoms indicate certain issues need exploration.

## PAUSE AND CONSIDER

**UNCOVERING WHAT** we don't know does not make us failures; it makes us awesome learners and gets us closer to co-creating fantastic outcomes with our stakeholders. Identifying what we need to learn helps us illuminate our unconscious biases and assumptions. We begin to see uncertainty as a guide toward action, and by focusing on which unknowns are most important, we prioritize our energy and resources on what we need to learn first. This work perfectly sets you up for the next skill of the PAUSE framework, Understand Stakeholders.

As we've discussed, no one likes uncertainty; we don't want to feel untethered or be biased, and it's stressful not to have all of the answers. But these are all part of our work in the social impact sector, and, really, part of each of our personal journeys. Consider these questions:

• How often would you say you encounter not knowing something? How does it make you feel? What do you do when you feel that way?

• What does your organization do when leaders and staff encounter uncertainty?

• How does it make you feel when I say that we are all biased and that we bring our biases to work? How do think bias shows up for you?

• How did it feel to brainstorm what you knew and didn't know about your challenge and stakeholder? How did it feel to prioritize your unknowns? Any "aha" moments or insights pop up for you?

# Understand Stakeholders

IT IS as simple *and* as difficult as this: If you don't understand stakeholders, how are you going to codesign life-changing solutions and create optimal value? This next skill of the PAUSE framework is the most complex. It is also a space where many of us who work in codesign hold tension.

The great part about understanding stakeholders is that you gain information and insights you never had before, and you can also validate (or just as enthusiastically, quickly invalidate) the direction in which you might be headed. You establish relationships, begin the process of working with stakeholders to cocreate potential solutions, and break through the status quo of how problems in silos and separation are typically addressed.

Unfortunately, there is also a bad part: many people will dip their pinky toe into the sea of potential learning and think that's enough. Understanding stakeholders and the work of empathy interviewing is often treated as a check box and feels transactional, like, "Okay, we talked to twenty people, now let's build!" At its worst, how information is gained from stakeholders is harmful, extractive, and tokenistic, and it ignores the rooted systems at play.

There is an empathy deficit not only on our planet but also in the sector. I think we have sometimes skipped being more connected, more empathetic, and more relational as a way to remove ourselves from accountability. As social impact professionals and organizations, we have assumed love and altruism, but if we were to talk to stakeholders, they might share that some of the work we have done and are doing is creating harm. This would mean that some organizations would have to consider how their competitive natures create suffering, and many would have to answer for what they tout as impact being wholly insufficient to make sustainable and long-lasting change. For a sector whose purpose is to create social impact, we often do a poor job actually authentically listening to and integrating learning from and with our stakeholders.

One of the keys to change starts with social sector leaders and decision-makers. There has been extensive research that demonstrates that the higher (hierarchically) someone rises in an organization (and not just in social impact organizations), the lower their ability to show up empathetically. Research has also shown a correlation between increased wealth and decreased empathy. Executive teams and board members often have the least amount of contact with internal and external stakeholders to create opportunities for collisions, connection, learning, and codesign. Someone once shared with me that the closest their decision-makers get to "real" community members, specifically people of color, "is when they pay someone to do their yard work."

I have seen this disconnect firsthand when leaders join a team and conduct empathy interviews. They are often not only stunned by the brilliance and creativity of frontline staff but also disturbed after hearing the pain and struggle community members are experiencing. When you work on the frontlines, you usually talk to a variety of individuals every day.

You're connecting them to resources; you hear the obstacles and frustration they're experiencing; you know what they're trying to accomplish; and you're doing your very best to support them. You are carrying people from work home with you in your heart and mind, and they weigh on your spirit.

This is not to say that leaders don't care or worry about other individuals, but for many leaders, most of their days might revolve around administrative tasks: approving payroll, interviewing applicants, planning meetings, and having one-on-one meetings with potential donors or supporters. They're often in a very different place empathetically. That distance, coupled with the dynamics we've discussed of how leaders are expected to have answers and how, like most of us, they will create what they know, informed by their own biases and positionalities, makes it imperative that we use new skills to break through and shine a light on some of these potential disconnects.

Leaders can prevent and begin to heal this potential lack of understanding by investing in pausing and creating time, space, and support for connection inside and outside the organization. When we don't prioritize and practice empathy in our workplaces, it often shows up as weak empathy outside our organizations. When we don't dedicate time and effort to being empathetic, we can create anger, frustration, distrust, fear, and anxiety among our many internal and external stakeholders. While connecting may feel time-consuming to some, repairing relationships often requires much larger amounts of time, energy, conversation, and strategy. I've seen several organizations rarely pause to ask, listen, and learn; they just keep barreling through providing services. Guess what? When these organizations had new programs they wanted to explore, their stakeholders were even less engaged and supportive, and as a result, staff morale, community buy-in, the program's goals, and the organization's reputation were often negatively impacted.

Many organizations will say, "We don't have time to talk to stakeholders," and in my experience, this is a bogus excuse, especially when most of my small teams can talk with twenty stakeholders in just a few hours. There is always time to connect, but it must be a priority. Some people fear that by connecting with stakeholders they are giving them access to the "behind the curtain" workings of the organization. Others are concerned that if they listen, they will get feedback they don't want to hear or create the expectation that they will do something to respond to what they hear. I would question what is behind their curtain that they feel they need to hide, and what is it about transparency that creates the most discomfort.

There are three provocations that guide the third skill of the PAUSE framework, Understand Stakeholders. They are:

- What if we could understand stakeholders' perspectives?
- What if we could uncover the why?
- What if we could have insights into people's actions?

Before I dive deeper into discussing these provocations in the next chapter, I think it is first important to discuss empathy, its different forms, and what it is and isn't.

## Different Levels of Empathy

Empathy is complex, and there are several very important elements to consider when you are thinking about how you might understand another person's perspective.

*It is a myth that you can, through conversation or by mimicking another person's experience, truly understand what it is to be them.* We often hear about "walking in someone else's shoes," but I question if this is really possible. I like the idea that many share about how we need to "remove our own shoes before trying on another's," but I think there is tension and significant uncertainty within empathy that must be explored.

In an excellent article called "Stop Bastardizing Design with False Empathy," Ovetta Sampson, VP head of design machine learning and responsible artificial intelligence at Capital One, says, "As a black woman in America, I can tell you that few people in the world can know what it's like to 'walk in my shoes.' And if you think that the result of empathy in design is all about you trying to really understand what another person is going through while leaving you unchanged, then you are an empathy offender."

In the article, she goes deep into the many forms of empathy and how empathy transforms us. Sampson discusses the work of Daniel Goleman, who coined and defined the term "emotional intelligence," and the three levels of empathy.

> The first level is cognitive/intellectual empathy. This is the empathy most folks are familiar with and mistakenly refer to when talking about empathy in human-centered design. Cognitive or intellectual empathy occurs when we know what others feel and what they think. If you think about this in terms of the design process, this happens in the story telling phase. The "what we heard," phase of our design research shares. In this phase, designers talk to people, write down what they said and share photos and quotes to communicate what they heard. A lot of folks stop here and expect this to build empathy.

The second level of empathy is emotional empathy. Sampson writes, "This is when you feel physically along with the other person, or feel what they feel, as though their emotions were contagious. Empaths famously have this ability. But research shows though we're neurologically wired to have emotional empathy, that instinct can fade over time." As I shared in the discussion of how we show up in the sector, those who are more empathic can be worn out by repeated exposures to other people's needs, wants, and fears.

The third level of empathy is compassion empathy, or empathetic concern. This is the level of empathy that moves you to action, as you not only understand what someone is facing and how they feel, but you want to try to do something about it. You can listen and not be motivated to do anything, or you can listen and it lights a fire under you to be better, learn more, and cocreate. Think back to the Section 8 housing story. You can clearly see where the role of empathy and its different levels show up with the two interviewees, Charlie and Monica.

While our positionalities can limit walking in someone else's shoes, you can and should try to experience something similar to what stakeholders might be experiencing. Not in an attempt to convince yourself that you have achieved full understanding, but to create a deeper connection between what you hear and what you do to support that person. For example, when the financial collapse that was caused by COVID-19 hit the United States, more people than ever before had to navigate government websites, bureaucracies, and delays to apply for unemployment benefits and loans. Some said that, for the first time, it exposed many wealthier Americans to the painfully frustrating and demoralizing experiences that many community members have endured to gain access to government benefits.

If you cannot or have not experienced exactly what someone is experiencing, like applying for government benefits, you can still connect with the feelings of confusion and powerlessness. Maybe consider how you felt when you got your first loan from a financial institution, when you filled out your first job application, last did your own taxes, or maybe filed for divorce. You probably weren't sure whom to talk to, what questions to ask, what information to include and where, and you probably had some apprehension about the outcome. While the experiences and instances are different, the emotions are similar in many ways. You can add layers of imagination to this exercise if you envision that the only paperwork you can find is not in your first language and think of how you might solve the problem of finding support from someone to help you. Maybe consider what you might do if you had another significant barrier, such as lacking a social security number or ID. What do you do then? One response could be just thinking, "Yes, filling out paperwork can be confusing," and another could be to connect the dots of the emotions embedded in other people's experiences with something that was challenging, confusing, infuriating, and defeating for you.

Connecting empathetically is about opening your mind and embracing complexity. *At its root, empathy is about understanding that your perspective is just your own and that you are providing space for another person's experience and their truth to live alongside your own.* To be successful empathetically, you are not only connecting to a feeling within you that is the same or similar to the feeling of another person, but also detaching and untangling your own emotions and experiences from theirs. When you connect with stakeholders, you will hear stories, ideas, justifications, experiences, and explanations that might be very different from your own, and you must be open to challenging your own immediate judgments and assumptions. Without acknowledging this attachment-detachment dance, you might listen to the experience of another, unintentionally compare it to your own, form judgment, and potentially dismiss, undervalue, or even develop contempt for that person. Sadly, this happens every day and we are all guilty.

I experienced a gift when I first started doing this work that totally shifted my thinking about empathy. I was coaching a multiday event with an organization and there was a woman on a team who seemed really grumpy about having to be part of the training. She appeared distracted, short-tempered, and easily frustrated. My brain immediately went to judgment. I made the assumption that she was pulling back from the work. I judged that she was not participating in the ways I thought she should to really demonstrate commitment to the process. As the training continued, I decided to check in with her, so during a break, I strategically lined up next to her at the snack table and asked her how she was doing.

She told me it was her first day back from maternity leave. It was the first time she had left her infant in childcare, and she was in pain because she needed to pump breast milk and was trying to find a way to do that in the rapid flow of the workshop. She was feeling very mixed emotions: excitement about being back with her colleagues but also tremendous sadness and anxiety about being away from her baby. This interaction stopped me in my tracks and I have never forgotten the shame I felt at that moment as a fellow mother who has felt those very same feelings. I was so ashamed that my judgment had created a story about and for this woman when I was totally uninformed.

Just as we all are biased, we all need to do internal work before we can be positioned for optimal connection fueled by empathy. We must acknowledge that what we think we know about a person from what we see on the outside might be in no way connected to what is really going on with a person on the inside. There are many times when the joyful person I have shown to others masked pain, sadness, and grief, and I think this has been true at some point for most of us.

We must also do the work involved in experiencing the shame, disappointment, and discomfort we might feel when we misstep, as this is an essential piece of self-empathy and self-awareness, which are key to connecting empathetically with others. I felt awful and was so angry with myself after I had wrongfully judged this new mother, but I sat with and processed those feelings, and the experience imprinted a powerful lesson I will never forget. None of us is perfect empathetically, but when we do the work to hone our empathy skills, not only will our potential solutions and organizations be elevated, but we will also be transformed.

## What Empathy Is and Isn't

### Connecting Empathetically Is Not about Connecting Sympathetically

Brené Brown has a well-known YouTube video called "Brené Brown on Empathy" in which she talks about how empathy is very different from sympathy. Empathy fuels connection and sympathy drives disconnection. She goes on to describe the work of Theresa Wiseman, a nursing scholar who has named the four qualities of empathy.

1 Perspective taking—the ability to take the perspective of another person or recognize their perspective as their truth

2 Staying out of judgment

3 Recognizing emotion in others

4 Communicating back the emotion you see

Brown says that empathy is feeling *with* people. Sympathy is more like seeing something that is messed up and saying, "Hmm, that looks rough," and then going back to what you were doing. It's also like feeling that something is wrong "over there," with "those people," and not right here, right now, urgently driving you to explore action. This is yet another reason why the sector must dismantle disconnects between those who hold the most institutional power and those who are closest to pain and potential solutions. Our positionality and biases separate us from one another and often nurture sympathetic rather than empathetic responses.

### Connecting Empathetically Is about Active Listening

The other very important skill that is essential to being a good human *and* a good empathetic stakeholder interviewer is being an active and empathetic listener. In 2021, I took part in an experience created by Edwin Rutsch, founding director of the Center for Building a Culture of Empathy, on how to lead empathy circles. I spent many hours over many weeks with total strangers all around the globe learning how to practice empathetic and active listening. It is a great way to stretch your level of comfort, as learning to listen is very difficult, especially in our fast-moving world where we are rapidly extracting snippets to match our own experiences and beliefs.

I consider myself a great listener; many think the same of themselves. We think we're good friends people can turn to. We might feel that we're empathetic, or even empathic, but I have learned that while you might feel you are a great listener, how you *demonstrate the act of listening* is more important. It's more than listening to hear, and way more than listening to respond; it's really about listening with the intent to understand and be able to nearly repeat what you heard another person say. In this training, we practiced extensively saying things like, "What I'm hearing you say is . . ." and then rephrasing or repeating what someone had just said without any introduction of a question, judgment, or the film of our own biases. I not only practiced these skills but also led about a dozen others in learning the practice, which was so eye-opening and reinforced that this is a skill we all need to improve.

I emphasize the importance of great listening (and great note-taking) not only because I have learned a lot from personally conducting hundreds of empathy interviews, but also because I have had years of experience watching interviews being conducted by team members. One early and alarming trend I noticed repeatedly was that when team members heard a person's answer to a question, they wrote quick summary statements in an attempt to capture all that was shared. When they went through their notes and pulled out key takeaways to share with their team, they said things like, "What they meant was…," "What they were trying to say was…," or "They were really talking about…" Even though we were present in the same interview, what I heard and the insights I identified were very different from those of the team members.

Interviews are not the time for interpretation. They are a time to deeply listen and thoroughly document, just as the words are spoken, not filtered through the biased lens of the listener. It is also super tempting during an interview to interrupt or jump in to start brainstorming ideas with the stakeholder, but this is not the time. Empathy interviews are about establishing a connection, making someone feel heard, and learning as much as possible. It is also not time to address inaccuracies or other negative feedback that might be shared. For example, if a stakeholder shares that your organization doesn't provide any resources online, and you know that your organization just spent $20,000 and six months launching an updated website, you just nod and write down, "Stakeholder said that we don't provide any resources online." No matter how tempting, you do not want to say, "We *do* have a site; it's right here, and we just spent a lot of money making it better!"

Your job is to listen to their experiences and then connect what you hear with all of your other learning. What you learn will help you make some early conclusions, and you will begin to explore and test some ideas around potential solutions. Because of our discomfort, we often fall into the trap of wanting to jump in or start to solve the problem, but we are there to remain quiet, listen, and learn.

### Connecting Empathetically Is Not about Surveys and Focus Groups

This statement bums people out and even makes some people mad. They say, "What do you mean we can't do focus groups and surveys?!" My response is that there are no empathy shortcuts, and I think that while both surveys and focus groups can give cues to action, they often generate kind of vanilla results and learning. If you insist on using them, I encourage you to be clear on your goal: their purpose is to signal where to focus your efforts but not be the be-all and end-all to sourcing feedback, information, data, and whatever else.

Many times, focus groups and surveys show the surface level of what people are thinking, saying, feeling, and doing. We often don't think we have time to connect one-on-one, so we use these shortcuts to provide clarity, and unfortunately, we often fill the gaps in our knowledge with assumptions and presumptions of *why* people think, say, feel, and do what they do. For example, let's say you get some survey results and you learn that 67 percent of people who responded are "somewhat satisfied" with your program. What do you do with that? How would you turn that data into any sort of significant learning that helps you understand the value you create for people or why they provided that response?

I know that when I complete surveys I'm often frustrated when a question is confusing and I want to ask someone for clarification about what they're trying to ask. Or, for another question, I might feel like I could write an entire thesis as an answer, but instead, I have to choose from four multiple-choice options or answer "yes" or "no." Surveys might give you an indication of where you need to focus your efforts to address additional uncertainty and where you may want to shape questions to learn more, but I find them incomplete and inadequate for empathetic connection and getting to "why."

Focus groups are often seen as the next best attempt at shortcutting empathy. I joke that focus groups are an introvert's nightmare and an extrovert's dream. They are risky for generating group think, where everyone just starts to agree with the prevalent belief in the room, and while you might gather a couple of interesting quotes or a few takeaways, it's really hard to get to "why" when you're in a shared space. It's inappropriate and awkward in front of everyone else to keep asking one individual why they feel the way they do and go deeper. In a group, it is much more difficult to make an empathetic connection and listen empathetically than if you spend time one-on-one with another person.

One of the things I love most about conducting empathy interviews is that you can hear people's stories behind what they are thinking, saying, feeling, and doing. You can go deeper, ask for clarification, and follow the breadcrumbs in a conversation that might lead to the unexpected.

In the next chapter, you will learn step-by-step how to craft your interview questions, how to conduct quality interviews, and how to really identify and then organize all of the wonderful learning you gather.

### Connecting Empathetically Is about Ethical Consent

I did not want to move on from this chapter without briefly touching on another key aspect of learning with stakeholders: ethical consent. Because in this codesign work there are often many dynamics at play that can unintentionally buttress and replicate harmful power dynamics, it is crucial to pause and include practices that provide full decision-making power to stakeholders. As George Aye, cofounder and director of innovation at Greater Good Studio, astutely points out, the design community does not currently have an official code of ethics for codesigning with stakeholders, internal or external. There are no standards for practice, licensing and accreditation, or continued education in both the traditional design and social impact design professions, like there are for other disciplines. There is no real accountability or oversight body, and as a result of this gray area, empathy can drift toward exploitation. Just as I have shared about the importance of outcomes over intent—and, hopefully, since you have now considered your positionality and biases and how they intersect with power—I want you to consider how these ethical elements impact your work, and how right now we each have a scenario that George refers to as "BYOE"—"Bring Your Own Ethics." I want you to question: What ethics do I/we "bring"? What ethical principles do I/we support, and which do we actually enforce and how? How do I/we address harm that can potentially be created when we engage in codesign?

Before you begin your outreach activities to plan and schedule interviews, define specifically what consent means. In my earlier work, consent meant "Okay, they said yes to being interviewed, so let's go. Question 1…" My thinking and knowing now is that we must explicitly define consent and people must clearly know what they are consenting to. This consent is also not just a one-time thing; consent continues and evolves as your relationship with the stakeholder evolves. Consent can be revoked, refused, and reconsidered at any time. My thinking about consent and the implications and strategies of building rapport with stakeholders has been in some part informed by the work of Tad Hirsch, professor of Art + Design at Northeastern University, and his article, "Practicing Without a License: Design Research as Psychotherapy."

The following are just a few key components of the discussion that we need to have with our potential interviewees. We must share

- our intentions and what we are trying to learn;

- who we are and what our role is in the project/organization;

- that to talk to us is entirely voluntary;

- that the person can choose to stop or pause sharing at any time;

- that if they are upset by anything they are sharing, we have resources to help;

- how their privacy or confidentiality will be protected;

- that we don't know what will result from their sharing with us (we cannot make any promises of outcomes or future resources); and

- that they can reach out to us in the future or we will connect to share what we have learned.

This consent must of course be provided in the language and format that the interviewee chooses, and all interactions are scheduled and conducted at the convenience and comfort of the stakeholder.

In all of our interactions, the stakeholder has the true power because without their input, stories, and feedback, we are left using traditional and ineffective methods that design weak and wasteful solutions. I would also argue that by recognizing that the power lies with and within stakeholders, we can shift how we show up as individuals and institutions and help mitigate harmful practices.

The last piece I want to highlight with relation to ethical consent is the issue of trauma and trauma-responsive design.

Rachael Dietkus, founder of Social Workers Who Design, is one of the leading voices in reshaping how we codesign solutions by integrating social work values, design research methods, and trauma-informed care principles. Rachael has informed much of my thinking and curiosity connected to trauma.

When you ask someone to share their stories with you, you are asking them to trust you enough to share deeply personal experiences. You are asking them in many cases to revisit their pain, confusion, frustration, and potential trauma. Your intent in asking questions is to learn so that you can potentially improve someone's life, but the unintended outcome might be someone feeling overwhelmed, upset, or a wide variety of other emotions, both anticipated and unexpected.

At this point, you may be pausing to think, as I did after taking a class led by Rachael, about all the times you interviewed and interacted with stakeholders and perhaps witnessed sadness, anger, frustration, and defeat. I want to share a story about one of these really difficult interactions that I've never forgotten from years back. I was working with a team that was interviewing individuals experiencing homelessness about their toileting behaviors. This is obviously a very sensitive topic for an abundance of reasons. The team was interviewing one individual and when she was discussing her experience, she became very frustrated. I still remember that at one point, she said, "I don't want to go to a shelter, I don't want a brochure with resources, and I don't want any government benefits. What I want is a plane ticket to go home." She shared that she had come to the US with her past partner, and since that relationship had dissolved, she just wanted to return to her home country to be back with her family but lacked the money to pay for the international flight. All we had to offer her was some food and the same type of resources she'd just said she did not want. We did not have funding for a plane ticket, or an organization at the tip of our fingers we could refer her to. I still feel shame and deep regret when I think back on this interaction because I feel like we let the community member down. Because we were "the organization," we had the power to be unprepared and the power to just "move on" to our next interview.

You might be thinking to yourself, "My challenge is about the best way to streamline a contract routing process. Is there really trauma there?" I don't know the answer, of course, and some challenges and topics are clearly more sensitive than others, but whatever is the delicate nature of the challenge at hand, there are three key aspects of ethical consent I want to emphasize—in full acknowledgment that for each of these topics, there are many experts and resources. I suggest you explore them.

First, it is essential to name and fully recognize that in some instances, you might be creating a setting in which you could cause or recreate trauma, and you need to be prepared to respond and provide resources that can actually help. Second, it is key to lead with what Rachael and others refer to as compassionate inquiry, and we all must make a commitment to build our trauma literacy and learn ways to more authentically and ethically connect with others, noticing both the discomfort of others and our own discomfort, and again respond in ways that help, not harm. Last, as the interviewer, it is key to also recognize that we all carry trauma from myriad sources, personal and professional, and what you hear might bring up feelings of trauma that *you* have experienced, also called vicarious or secondary trauma. These feelings might influence your ability to actively listen, and you may also need resources and support to process the emotions and thoughts that are stirred up as a result of the interview(s).

**UNDERSTANDING ANOTHER** person or group of people is so complex and multifaceted. It requires work and dedication to authentically connect to other people. I hope you recognize the value of grounding in and accounting for ethical consent.

We are so busy that sometimes we either gloss over empathetic connection and listening or dip a teeny bit into it and call it a day. It is imperative that before you begin this work of interviewing, you understand that 1) the definition of empathy itself varies greatly, 2) there are different kinds of empathy, 3) your positionality and biases impact how you apply empathy to your work, and 4) ethical consent must be clearly defined and secured when working with stakeholders, and should also include provisions to prevent and respond to trauma and retraumatization.

Empathy is a space of tension, but it is also filled with opportunities. You are on a learning journey and I want you to be changed by what you learn. I hope you will embrace the tension, activate your self-awareness and self-empathy, and carry the stories you gather with you into your personal and professional lives. Consider these questions:

- How well do you think you understand your different internal and external stakeholders?

- How does your organization provide time and resources to support learning about the experiences of stakeholders?

- Have you ever seen examples of harm that were caused internally or externally when there was a lack of empathy in an organization?

- Consider this statement by Ovetta Sampson: "If you think that the result of empathy in design is all about you trying to really understand what another person is going through while leaving you unchanged, then you are an empathy offender." How does it make you feel? What do you think of the term "empathy offender"? How do you imagine you might be changed by learning about the experiences of others?

- Author Daniel Goleman's third level of empathy, compassion empathy, or empathetic concern, is when you are moved by what you hear and take action. Do you remember a time when you experienced this? What moved you and why? What action did you take?

- A very important skill for empathy interviewing is active and empathetic listening. Have you ever experienced an active listening exercise? How skilled do you think you are at active listening?

- How frequently do you use surveys and focus groups to collect information from stakeholders? How are these put together? What are the benefits and limitations that they've provided? Are there issues, concerns, problems, and/or opportunities you've identified into which you want or need to go deeper?

- What considerations, processes, and protections does your organization have to ensure ethical consent in your work with stakeholders? How do you incorporate considerations of trauma and trauma-responsiveness?

# 10

# Gaining Insights into People's Actions

W E OFTEN don't take the time to understand *why* people do what they do. We usually just ask what people think they will do or listen to what they say they will do. It is imperative that we understand why people say the things they say and do the things they do because that is how we're actually going to address problems. Most people don't just run around in circles waving their hands in the air when they have a problem; they come up with solutions. It is so important to understand what people need, what they have tried, and why those solutions worked or didn't, because that will also inform how we make progress. One-on-one interviews are the best way to understand someone's actions, and there are many nuances I will discuss.

When you ask people how they are, how well something is working or not, or what they might need, they might say, "I'm fine" or "It's fine." There could be many reasons for the quick answer, but in most instances, even when you're greeting a friend with a "Hi, how are you?" and they reply with an "I'm fine" (as appropriate, of course), you might ask follow-up questions. This opportunity to go deeper to achieve additional understanding is also true for empathy interviews. One of my favorite stories shows how if you move past "just fine," you can unlock tremendous opportunities.

There was a large organization that provided pass-through federal funding to a large number of nonprofits in one community. The organization formed a team and decided that they would pause and really look at their invoicing process. Every month, partner agencies that received funding would submit an invoice for payment, which the organizations relied on to make their payroll and cover their expenses. The team from the large oversight organization knew that their process had been flawed for more than a decade, but they had never taken the time to pause to see how it might be improved.

When the team first began conducting their interviews and asked people what they thought of the invoicing process, many people said, "It's fine." The team realized that the passive responses might be due to the asymmetrical power at play between what was essentially "the funder" and "the recipient." For their next interviews, the team made sure to "disarm politeness" and made it very clear that the feedback shared would in no way impact their financial relationship. They really wanted open and honest information. To improve the feedback they received, they also asked if they could watch some people complete the invoicing process so that they could see the steps involved.

One woman, "Francisca," who had said the process was fine earlier, showed the team how difficult it was to navigate the required paperwork. She shared that for years she had been the only person in her entire organization who knew how to complete the process. Because of the complexity and her integral role, performed the first week of every month, she had missed weddings, funerals, and vacations because she did not want to jeopardize the financial security of her colleagues and organization. The team was horrified by the outcomes their negligence and passivity had caused, and they were motivated to do something about it.

The driving force and the goal the team committed to was creating a process that would let Francisca take time off the first week of any month. After some additional interviews with other people in similar roles, and finding a brilliant frontline staff member who turned out to be a spreadsheet whiz, they were able to test multiple invoicing form prototypes and re-design the invoicing process. After just a matter of months, the team calculated that across their one community they were saving their partners eight hundred hours a month! The team became driven to imagine all the ways that they were unintentionally using up time, energy, and resources of their agency partners and they started looking at other elements of their systems, including their annual contract renewal process.

Beyond accepting "it's fine" as an answer, another trap we can fall into when conducting empathy interviews is asking people to predict their future actions. We often ask questions like, "If you were to _____ , how would you do/solve _____ ?" or "If I offered you _____ , do you think you would use/like it?" Unfortunately, most people are terrible at predicting their future behavior and often what they say they will or would do is not reflective of the real actions they will eventually take.

For example, if you went to a caregiver and said, "If you were trying to find early childhood education resources for your child, what would you do?" They might say that they would go online and do a search, talk to family and friends, and look through a local magazine to see if there were advertisements or feature stories about resources. Basically, they might have really lovely descriptions and ways they would seek support. In reality, it may look like starting an online search and then becoming distracted when a kiddo needs a diaper change; or trying to talk to a friend about early childhood resources and it turning into a larger, more important discussion about potty training; or having a quick glance in a magazine that shows just what you want, but then there are unexpected hurdles when making contact with one of the resources. The point is, there are always more opportunities for someone to walk you through all the steps they actually took, their real actions, to help you see obstacles and opportunities, and gain clarity.

What's more generative is to ask, "The last time you looked for early childhood education resources, what did you do and was it helpful?" Let's say they share about their online search for information. You want someone to walk through all the potential variations of their actual experience, such as: "I went to X website and clicked the link for more information, but the link was broken," or "I saw X, but I was really looking for Y," or "The website looked really weird on my phone because it wasn't optimized for smartphones," or "I downloaded the form but my printer ran out of ink so I wasn't able to complete it," or "I found this great checklist of what to consider and it was super helpful!" Someone walking you through their *actual* experience is much more powerful than a prediction of what might happen.

## Getting to Great Questions

The key to empathy interviewing is story. We want our stakeholders to trust us enough that they will share what it is like to walk through their day. We want them to share their experiences openly and honestly so we can identify each of the different opportunities to create value. Through their stories (and trust), we can better understand the actions people are currently taking or have taken, learn what's working and what's not, and move beyond words to action.

The first step to crafting great questions is to look at the most crucial unknowns you identified in the Assess Uncertainty skill of the PAUSE framework. Just as you prioritized what you needed to learn, you need to prioritize what you want to ask. You may have only twenty minutes to spend with someone, so instead of asking just any sort of question you're curious about, you need to make sure you're asking the most important questions that will help you learn about your most important areas of uncertainty (sometimes as quickly as possible, if the stakeholder has limited time). You are essentially taking your greatest unknowns, prioritizing them, and turning them into questions.

There are a few important elements of a good empathy question. The first is that your questions should be mostly, if not all, open-ended because the goal of the interview is to hear stories from people and really get to the "why."

I created this example table when I was training a group of journalists on how to do empathy interviews. This was hilarious to me because I assumed that journalists would be super awesome at asking people questions—that's literally a major part of what they do for a living. It turned out they needed a helping hand to go deeper.

The point of this side-by-side is to illustrate that empathy interviews should really be a conversation. While you are trying to complete as many quality interviews as you can so you have good information from which to brainstorm potential solutions, you're also working from a space of compassionate curiosity.

| Gather Information | Hear Stories |
|---|---|
| How long have you been a partner? | How long have you been a partner? |
| Would you consider renewing your partnership? | What has your experience been like overall? |
| With which other organizations do you partner? | What has been the best experience you've had being our partner? |
| | What has been the worst experience you've had? |
| | Can you give me an example of a partnership that you enjoy and that has been extremely valuable? Why do you think this is the case? |

In the left column, the questions are examples of those someone might ask if they're simply gathering basic information. If you look at the three questions on the left, the stakeholder might provide answers like, "six years," and "yes," and share the names of three other organizations.

When you look at the right side of the table, you can see the difference in questions, those someone could ask to draw out stories, get to the "why," and form a more powerful connection to people's experiences. The first question, "How long have you been a partner?" is the same in each column, but the follow-up questions matter: "What has your experience been like overall? . . . What has been the best experience you've had being our partner? . . . What has been the worst experience you've had?" As you can see, those are very different questions that will generate very different answers. In fact, "what's the best" and "what's the worst" are two of my favorite questions, especially if you're talking about a program or service and asking people for feedback about what's really great and what needs improvement.

The next question—"Can you give me an example of a partnership that you enjoy and that has been extremely valuable? Why do you think this is the case?"—asks the stakeholder to think beyond the existing relationship (especially since the interviewer now knows what they consider to be the good and bad about their organization), and now the interviewer is learning about what they might consider to be the "gold standard." They are learning about the bar that's been set to which they, and the value they provide, might be compared.

The questions could then continue and go deeper or become more specific if time allows. You typically begin with overarching questions like, "What has your experience been like overall?" and then you can get more specific and learn more about issues, such as their onboarding experience and the tools and resources they use and need, and gain feedback on a specific program or event. In my experience, most interviews last about thirty minutes, so you must prioritize the top questions you want to ask (including follow-up questions), knowing that you can include additional questions and get more specific as time allows.

Think back to the most important unknowns for the caregiver example.

- Where are the best places to reach caregivers?

- Where are caregivers going for early childhood caregiving support?

- What do caregivers need and want?

- What are caregivers' greatest priorities?

- What barriers are there for caregivers participating in services?

Each of these unknowns can be easily transformed into questions, such as:

- Think about an average week. Where do you spend most of your time? Where are you going, and what are you doing? What about on a typical weekend?

- Can you think of the last time you were looking for support or resources for your child? What did you need? Where did you look? Was it beneficial? Why or why not?

These are just some brief examples of questions you could similarly craft for your most important unknowns in a matter of minutes. There are many, many ways to craft questions, so the key is not to overthink it or get stuck on wordsmithing, but to just get started. Your questions are a tool that will evolve as you conduct interviews and your learning grows. It is important to also leave space for what emerges in your conversations because sometimes a stakeholder will say something totally unexpected or introduce a really important topic or aspect of the challenge that you've never before considered. Document those statements and feel encouraged to continue to ask questions to learn more.

So, after looking at your prioritized unknowns, what questions could you ask stakeholders? Don't forget to make your questions open-ended, to prioritize questions in case of limited time, and to start with broad questions that can later get more specific.

Because I have conducted hundreds of empathy interviews (and really love it), I have an abundance of suggestions and tips on how to identify whom to talk to, how to track your interviews, considerations for who should ask the questions, and much more, all on my book website, NoMoreStatusQuo Book.com.

## Identifying Key Insights

So, after you've completed one or more interviews, the first step to identifying key insights is to have very good interview notes. You should have typed or handwritten notes (they need to be legible for you and your team, if applicable) from each interview. These interview notes should also be stored in a safe physical or virtual documentation space for future reference. Ensure you protect stakeholder confidentiality in whatever ways were promised in your consent process.

When you take notes from an interview, I want you to make as close to a transcript of the exact words that are spoken as possible. By doing this, you help remove potential bias and your own personal filtering. It is your job to listen accurately and collect the correct information. After each interview (and before you begin another one), it is helpful, when possible, to take a few minutes to clean up your handwriting or typing and double-check your notes to make sure they make sense to you and anyone else who might need to access them. Make sure you have captured to the best of your ability what the stakeholder shared.

Go through your now very clean and easy-to-understand notes and add stars, circles, highlights, and/or comments to indicate key takeaways. You can also pull out these key takeaways and list them as bullet points at the end of your notes, or add them on physical or virtual sticky notes, one takeaway per sticky note. This is an efficient way to prepare for sharing your learning with others, rather than having to use time reading through all of your notes.

There are a few elements to consider when you are analyzing your notes for key takeaways.

- **What signals did the stakeholder give you about how they were feeling?** Sometimes people show you the depth of their feelings through their body language, which is a large part of communication. This body language can vary significantly based on the cultural background and comfort of the stakeholder, but I want you to reflect on whether you noticed any changes. For example, when you asked a question, did the person get animated, talk more loudly, sit up, and/or appear angry or excited about their answer? Or did they exhale a deep sigh and drop their shoulders as maybe a sign of defeat, sadness, or hopelessness?

- **What is all the new information you acquired?** Did you learn anything that answered a question or addressed an area of uncertainty?

- **Were there things the stakeholder said that were different from what you expected to hear?**

- **What else do you need to learn?** During the interview, did you uncover any new information that generated additional questions and new unknowns? This should be documented along with any edits, changes, and additions to your interview script so that they can potentially be integrated into future interviews and collected and shared to demonstrate important learning moments.

- **Did any themes or patterns emerge?** After you talked to a handful of people, did you notice that the same or a very similar response was mentioned multiple times? It's important to document the themes that emerge; they are signals for where to focus your future efforts.

Sometimes you've got to talk to people back-to-back, so you can wait to clean up and analyze your learning until you've completed all of your interviews. This clean-up time is important because so many wonderful and really important details can get lost in the shuffle.

If you can, try to pull out some direct quotes you can share with others. These quotes don't need to be attributed to anyone (especially if you want or need to protect stakeholders' privacy and anonymity), but they can be helpful in conveying the emotion, context, and urgency behind an interview that others were not there to witness. It can be difficult to convey empathy to someone who wasn't conducting the interview with you, but if you can impart the *stories* that were shared by the stakeholder, it can leave a strong impression and you can better communicate the power of the interview.

### What Identifying Insights Looks like with Your Team

Interviewing is usually a one-on-one or two-person task, but when you are working as part of a team, you need to share all of your learning from your independent work. Each team member should share their key takeaways and group them into similar themes. These collective key takeaways will drive the next step of the PAUSE framework, Solution Testing.

## Going Further: Empathy and Understanding Stakeholders

Now that you have cleaned up your notes and teased out key takeaways, it is essential to pause to expand beyond just what you heard and to address the limitations of cognitive, or intellectual, empathy. Take time to sit with (and even meditate on) what you heard and felt, and try to reach the second level of empathy, emotional empathy, where you connect to an emotion you have experienced that relates to what you heard the stakeholder express. It's ideal if you can go even deeper to the third level and experience compassion empathy, or empathetic concern, and see in what ways you feel moved to take action based on what you learned. The next step of the PAUSE skills, Solution Testing, is intended to take the insights and inspiration you gained and explore potential solutions to codesign with stakeholders.

As I mentioned above, I have an abundance of additional content on my book website that goes deep into the specific details of empathy interviewing, but I want to share a few additional and essential components here.

### Follow Up with Stakeholders

As a last question of the interview, you should consider asking permission to recontact the stakeholder in the future, when applicable. After you gain this initial permission, you should get renewed consent and continue to engage stakeholders in the learning process, especially to ask follow-up questions, conduct additional empathy interviews, and seek their feedback when you get to the Solution Testing phase.

Staying connected is also a great way to update stakeholders on the progress of your learning, even if you decide to pivot. This can help the stakeholder understand that you actually paid attention to what they shared and will pursue potential actions, or that their feedback provided key learning that led you in some different directions (note: how you follow up with stakeholders should also align with what you shared in your consent process before you conducted your interviews).

I think people intrinsically have an expectation or hope that the information they shared will be helpful or lead to something. When you keep in touch, you not only deepen your relationship and gain additional insights, but also counter the typical extractive behavior of conducting interviews with stakeholders and then never re-engaging with them. By losing connection, stakeholders may never see the outcomes their feedback helped create, and it might feel like all of that time and energy was wasted, which can result in increased mistrust and reluctance for any future engagement with your organization, or any organization.

### Say Thank You and Compensate People

It is very important to say thank you again and again to the amazing stakeholders who have contributed so much to your learning and from whose feedback you are able to test and codesign potential solutions. I, and most of the teams I work with, am usually blown away by how gracious and vulnerable people are in sharing their experiences.

Beyond a thank you and a warm, fuzzy feeling, you also need to compensate people for sharing their feedback. It is super common in the sector for community members especially to *not* be paid for their time and insights, and this needs to change to further address inequities and harmful power dynamics in the sector. As often as possible and as many times as necessary, provide money, gift cards, food, and/or something else of value to your super helpful interviewees.

### Empathy Is Never "Done"

The number one question I get about empathy interviewing is, "How do I know when I'm done?" People want to know, specifically, what number of stakeholders they need to talk to and when they can stop. To this question, I must provide an unsatisfactory answer: "It depends." *I* know I can stop interviewing when I hear the same information, insights, and ideas repeatedly. When I hit this sweet spot, it signals to me that I have sourced the majority of the insights that I can gather from stakeholders at that moment and it is time to shift to brainstorming potential solutions. The key is quality over quantity because your goal is to gain deep understanding. Be more motivated by learning than by talking to as many people as possible.

While empathy itself can in some ways act as an "intervention," generating feelings of appreciation and respect in stakeholders (especially when you have never talked to the stakeholders before *and* you provide compensation), people often tend to treat empathy as a check box. The reality is that you are never "done" with empathy because it should drive everything you do. Your goal should be to create the most value possible, and you can do that only if you understand, and communicate and cocreate with stakeholders—so, really, you're never done.

Empathy is intertwined with all of the skills of the PAUSE framework, and my hope is that you will use your empathy skills in your daily personal and professional lives. Empathy is always a choice and one of the best tools you can use in uncertainty. When you feel like you're bumping up against something you don't understand, it's time to go learn using your empathy skills. When you're having a debate or misunderstanding with another person, my best advice is to lean on empathy. When these and other moments arise, pause and see if you can gain clarity through connection. Be specific about what you need to learn and the questions you need to ask, and how you can learn from and with people who might be closest to the answers.

You can listen to or read an article, or watch a video, but there is nothing like the energy you exchange when you sit with and listen to another person. I can still see the faces and hear the words of people I interviewed a decade ago because what they shared moved and motivated me so greatly. The work of empathy is rooted in evolution, growth, and learning. It's all a process of learning about yourself and expanding the way you see the world and how you think about people and your work.

I hope that empathy interviewing changes you. After each interview, I walk away with a new sense of connection to our collective humanity and my own evolving journey. I hope you think about your work differently and pause to reflect and interrogate your and your organization's practices. I'll leave you once more with the words of Ovetta Sampson: "The truth is, for empathy to be effective in design, we as designers have to engineer it on a daily basis. That means being in [a]constant mode of self-reflection about who we are and how we show up in the spaces and places we invade as designers."

## PAUSE AND CONSIDER

IT IS one of the greatest challenges to understand why people do what they do. When we ask respectful and well-crafted questions, we can experience the gift of people illuminating our thinking by sharing their experiences and feedback. It's in the interactions with other amazing humans that the light bulbs glow, our pulse races, and we say, "Oh! Now I get it!" I honestly got the chills just typing those words because I love those feelings of connection so much!

Now that you've learned how understanding stakeholders is much more involved than finding some people, asking some questions, extracting insights, and driving off into the sunset, my hope for you is that you will fall in love with the problems you want to address and become deeply committed to not only improving who you are as an ethical and empathetic interviewer but also connecting with others to codesign potential solutions. Consider these questions:

- Have you ever received or given an "it's fine"-type of response related to your work? How did it make you feel?

Did it make you wonder about unspoken feedback or was there feedback you wish you could have shared?

- Have you ever conducted a one-on-one interview with a stakeholder? If so, when was that and for what purpose? How did it go and what did you learn? If you haven't conducted one yet, why not?

- Are there favorite questions you like to ask when you are looking for feedback?

- As we've discussed, our positionalities, experiences, and biases impact how we see, interpret, and behave in the world. Are there ways you anticipate these elements will impact your interviews?

- Have you ever been interviewed by (or had a conversation with) a person who interrupted you or made the conversation more about them? How did that feel? Have you ever had a conversation when you felt really heard? How did that feel?

- How did it feel to look at your key unknowns and craft empathy interview questions? What about creating questions felt simple, and what about it felt more challenging?

- The ability to identify key insights varies by person and is a skill that you can grow over time. Thinking about your ability level right now, how prepared do you feel to listen to what people share and pull out the most important takeaways? What do you hypothesize you might need to improve these skills?

# 11

# Are You Still Aligned?

JUST AS I hope that empathy interviewing changes you, I also hope it informs your decision-making. Before we move on to the fourth PAUSE skill, Solution Testing, and discuss the best ways to brainstorm, prioritize, and test potential solutions, you need to pause to determine where you are with our challenge and stakeholder.

This is a very important pause point in your learning journey and you have considerations, conversations, and decisions to make. When you began your journey with the first step of the PAUSE framework, Package the Challenge, you got more clarity and alignment by drafting your hypothesis of the challenge and selecting a stakeholder. These were your first guesses of what the problem was and who was most impacted, and you had not yet made contact with stakeholders for one-on-one interviews. As we know, what we think will happen is sometimes off, and this can be true of your challenge and stakeholder selection as well.

The great news is that now you have interviewed numerous stakeholders and identified key insights, and you have a much clearer sense of whether or not you are on the right track. Two ways to check your alignment is to look at what you (and if applicable, your team) wrote for the hypothesized quote(s) that you thought stakeholders would say about the challenge from their perspective. Think about all of the key takeaways you gathered from your interviews. Is what you heard aligned with what you hypothesized the stakeholders would say? In what ways was your learning similar or different?

You can also revisit your knowns and unknowns. Did what you heard in your interviews match what you thought you knew? Were any of those ideas challenged or affirmed? What about your unknowns? Do you now have new clarity *as well as* new unknowns?

If what you expected and heard are aligned, you can add nuances and keep moving ahead. If what you thought and what you heard are not aligned, focus on what is different. Is there something about the challenge or stakeholder (or even that potential solution you've had tucked in the back of your mind that you have yet to test) that now feels off? Is this still the challenge? Is this still the stakeholder most deeply impacted? Is this still what you need and/or want to focus on?

Remember that I said we must honor the struggle, winding path, and messiness of learning? You may feel like this pause point jolts you out of the momentum you have built from diving into your unknowns and enjoying your empathy interviews, but this is a pivotal moment. Let me share five examples that illustrate why it's so important to use this pause point and what you might realize now that you've conducted your empathy interviews.

**You're not addressing the correct challenge.** I worked with a city that wanted to focus on crime in a certain area of their community because based on statistics and 911 calls, there had been a noticeable and concerning increase. A team was formed that included law enforcement and other community representatives. They had the data, knew what symptoms they were seeing, identified their areas of uncertainty, and drafted their questions. When they conducted their interviews, totally unprompted, every single person shared that the most or more important challenge for them was affordable housing. Community members said they knew there was crime in their neighborhood, and some people said that they felt safe because they or their families had lived in those neighborhoods for generations. They felt very comfortable and confident knowing a majority of their neighbors. What they most wanted to discuss and get support with was affordable housing.

One community member shared a story about a drive-by shooting that occurred while she was walking her kids home from school. She talked about diving to cover their bodies, yet she, too, said that affordable housing was her biggest concern. Community members told the team about their absentee landlords, landlords raising rents by up to 30 percent per year, and fighting huge rodent and insect problems. Many shared that they would be facing potential homelessness if the rent increases continued. The team members were completely surprised by these responses. They did not expect to hear about housing; they were there to address crime.

The team decided to pivot and change the challenge on which they were focused. They paused to identify their new knowns and unknowns related to housing, drafted new questions, and completed additional interviews. They uncovered a total mismatch of some of their local programs with what was most needed by community members; they identified significant issues with their housing website and major process gaps in their housing resources; they revealed ways that absentee landlords were insulated from accountability; and they began exploring rent stabilization ordinances and other policy changes.

The data on crime and the anecdotal evidence from which the team was working made sense for their original challenge focus, but as the example illustrates, we often do not know the realities and priorities behind what our stakeholders are experiencing until we learn *from them*. This team exemplifies the humility and flexibility involved in learning. If you find that what you thought was the challenge is not the highest priority for stakeholders, it is important to pause and consider your resources and the strategic focus of your organization. If the challenge is connected to your mission and leaders want to support further work, then pursue the new challenge, prioritize new stakeholders (if needed), identify knowns and unknowns, write empathy interview questions, and conduct these conversations. If your organization cannot or does not want to focus on the new challenge, it would be ethical to connect with other community partners or agencies to share your learning and see how they can help.

**The solution you have in mind is way overbuilt.** As much as I ask that teams enter this process with a beginner's mind, it is human nature to address a challenge with a few solution ideas in tow. Sometimes, when you conduct empathy interviews you learn that the solution you have in mind may actually be overbuilt for the needs of stakeholders. I worked with a city that was focused on providing toilets for people experiencing homelessness in their downtown area. The impetus was increased reports of human waste in public spaces. The city imagined that they would use federal dollars to build a permanent restroom structure similar to one they had seen in another region. This was what I consider "the Cadillac of public toilets." It had specific lighting that would prevent the ability to find veins for drug injection, automated features to reduce overstaying, and a bunch of other bells and whistles.

What the team learned from talking to individuals experiencing homelessness was that their greatest restroom needs were between 10 p.m. and 6 a.m. During the day, most stakeholders shared that they had worked out very clear plans for which restrooms they would use when and where. The team also learned that there was a lot of movement and migration among the population of people experiencing homelessness, and that building a permanent structure would serve only a portion of the stakeholder community for a portion of the year. They learned that a few high-traffic existing public restrooms were extremely unclean, and stakeholders reported a lack of changing tables, which led to parents having to lay clothing and blankets on filthy restroom floors. They also learned that human waste in one area could be reduced if an old set of bus benches, which no longer received bus service, were removed.

Based on all that the team learned, they realized that the fancy bathroom idea was not what they needed to invest in. Instead, the bus benches were repurposed in other locations, saving the city resources, and the city determined that mobile restroom units that could move with stakeholders were a better fit, also saving resources by not building a permanent structure requiring water and sewer connections. The existing restroom that was in need of increased maintenance received a changing table and an improved cleaning schedule. Last, as part of the project, the team engaged downtown business owners to understand their perspectives and concerns, and they created a detailed map of the downtown area that showed all of the restrooms available for public use.

If this local government had built the "fancy toilet" anchored in one spot, it would have been a poor use of resources and the other, more comprehensive solutions could have been overlooked. If you find that the one solution you have in mind is way overbuilt, it is important to consider all of the comprehensive and "small" but impactful ways that you can create meaningful change.

**There is a better or different solution.** Sometimes we think we know what our stakeholders need most, but then, through interviews we are shifted in a whole new direction. I worked with an organization that helped adults get their GEDs. They noticed that their student retention numbers were down and thought that if they created an on-site childcare facility for students with children, those students could attend classes with fewer obstacles. This sounded very nice and seemed to make sense, but, of course, they needed to test this promising opportunity.

Interestingly, when the team interviewed past students who had stopped coming to classes, nearly every student asked if they could come back. The team was stunned and a little heartbroken by the request, but also excited because the organization desperately wanted all of their students to reach their personal goals, no matter what form their journey took. They hadn't realized that the students believed "once you're out, you're out," and that there was only one "right" way to get their GEDs. They learned that students left school for many different reasons, only a few related to classwork. When the team asked about childcare, most students reported having family, friends, and other childcare options, and that wasn't a strong pain point.

As a result, the team created a series of four vignettes that each highlighted a different student's journey to getting their GED. It showed all the ways in which people could stay, leave, and come back, and have support all along the way. The team incorporated these vignettes in their next orientation session, and the initial feedback from students was tremendous. Students reported feeling like the organization really cared about them, and that they had multiple support structures to help them reach their goals. Because they listened to their stakeholders, not only did the organization potentially save a substantial number of resources not building a childcare center, but also the program's retention numbers increased greatly in new student cohorts, and the team helped past students return to the classroom. Similar to the last example of an overbuilt solution, *it is essential to release any hold on what you think should be or what you want to be the solution; be open-minded to the directions in which stakeholders guide you.*

**You don't actually want to address that challenge.** Sometimes when you conduct empathy interviews you uncover more elements to the challenge than you imagined and you may decide that you don't want to use resources to move forward. An organization was considering deepening their focus on corporate philanthropy as a way to increase donations. This agency was in a community with some big-name companies, and they wanted to create new relationships and see if they could engage the companies and their corporate employees in volunteer opportunities and giving. After completing (and trying to complete) interviews with these different corporations, the agency came to understand that they were consistently hitting gatekeeping mechanisms that made relationship building difficult (e.g., being referred to a website, getting no response to emails, being asked to submit a grant rather than having a conversation).

They also noticed from their research and interviews that every couple of years, many corporations would change their community giving focus. The agency realized that this would put their investment in relationship building at risk because the corporation's connection to the mission could potentially dissolve. They also learned that many large corporations have their own staff, even a full department, who focus on employee engagement, volunteerism, and giving, and they did not need extra support from an outside entity.

After taking all of the learning under consideration and analyzing the resources they had available, the agency decided that moving forward was not the best idea. It is not a failure to decide that you don't want to work on the challenge you had in mind; it is a huge win and resources are saved! When you move on, it is very important to document and share your data and insights as evidence to support your decision. Sharing this information across different levels of the organization is powerful because 1) it helps people feel informed, 2) it may prevent that same idea from being pursued again the next year, and 3) it sends a signal to other staff that your organization listens to feedback and responds to data.

**You need to break the challenge down into manageable pieces.** Sometimes when you choose a challenge, you unknowingly take on more than you can handle. I was working with a local government that wanted to electrify their entire fleet of vehicles. The team knew this sounded like a large task, but when they dove in, they uncovered a huge number of moving parts and decided that there might be an opportunity to refine their challenge—they could focus on optimizing the existing fleet before jumping into a major infrastructure investment.

What they found by analyzing the data and conducting interviews was that in some instances there was one vehicle for every two employees and about seven hundred vehicles were driven fewer than three thousand miles per year. There was very little car sharing between departments because there was no mechanism in place to do so, and funding to replace older vehicles had been cut years before in a citywide budget slash. As a result, many staff were driving their own cars to have a more modern and reliable ride. The team also learned that many people were taking very short trips to complete inefficient tasks, like dropping off paper forms instead of using online platforms or scanning and emailing attachments. Some of the fleet vehicles were also used primarily seasonally, such as the large passenger vans that were mostly used by a summer program to transport young people.

As you can see, there is a lot to unpack just from their initial learning (and that's even after they had already simplified their challenge focus). The team realized that they needed to take even smaller bites and focus on one department at a time before they could branch out to the entire city. They realized that a one-size-fits-all solution would not be effective. They needed to do a deeper dive into each department to better understand their similar and different challenges, and they needed to focus their learning on shared issues that could apply across departments, such as improving interdepartmental communication, reducing unnecessary short trips, and investigating innovative and alternative transportation options like ridesharing or carpooling. If you need to split up your original challenge into smaller challenges and areas of focus, you simply then put the PAUSE skills back into action and begin your revised learning journey.

**There are many directions your learning can take you.** Instead of plowing ahead and potentially creating "giant triangles of waste," we build in pause points like this to analyze where we are and make important decisions about next steps. Can you imagine if any of the above examples were just built from an idea and no stakeholder interviews were conducted? These stories exemplify why I often ask, "Do you want the hot mess now or later?" because at some point you will encounter that learning moment when you realize that you've got it "wrong" or taken on too much, or you need to pass on a project. It is so much better to make these realizations in days or weeks versus several months or years.

Learning is messy and convoluted and requires flexibility. Sometimes it can feel frustrating and as if you are going "back to zero" when you need to reconsider your challenge and stakeholder, but you (and your team, if applicable) will be able to move quickly and efficiently to gain new learning, and, honestly, these are some of the most important learning moments you can experience. Pausing to analyze, think critically, and reground increases everyone's awareness, especially that of leadership, that there are numerous assumptions and uncertainties embedded within every program, service, and project, and it is up to all of us to respond to the needs of our stakeholders. Showing vulnerability and learning in action can inspire other people across your organization to show up and do their work differently, reinforcing the fact that learning, not just building, is a key value of your organization.

Just like when you completed the first PAUSE skill, Package the Challenge, your intent here was to get aligned before moving forward. The same is true of your next steps: exploring and testing potential solutions. You need to be clear on and aligned with your learning so that you (and your team) are ready to explore how you might address your challenge.

## PAUSE AND CONSIDER

**LIKE THE** organization that showed its students the many ways in which they could complete their GED, I hope you, too, feel supported, inspired, and validated as you consider all the diverse roads you can take based on the knowledge you gained from stakeholder interviews. If you need to leave your previously held challenge behind or change or revise your challenge or stakeholder, or if you feel affirmed and excited to keep going, all of the learning you've gained so far is a tremendous success! You have trusted the process and tried out some new skills, and I hope you see how much you can learn to inform your decisions in a short amount of time.

If you are now recentered and ready to move forward, you are perfectly positioned to explore potential solutions. As you've put your flexibility and self-awareness to the test, you will have more opportunities to stretch further and test your beliefs. Consider these questions:

- It's hard sometimes to have to pause and re-examine your work. How did it feel to reflect on where you started and compare that to what you have learned so far?

- Could you relate to any of the examples shared? Did you encounter any of these shifts with your current learning or when trying to address other challenges in the past?

**12**

# Solution Testing

W E HAVE arrived at one of my favorite skills of the PAUSE framework, and for many, this is the moment you've been waiting for: Solution Testing. *Unfortunately, solution brainstorming is the stage at which most status quo problem-solving work in the sector mistakenly begins.* Most people see a problem and jump to brainstorming; I hope you are now convinced of the value of engaging stakeholders first and committing to codesign on your learning journey.

The fourth skill of the PAUSE framework, Solution Testing, includes two steps. The first step is focused on these three provocations.

- What if we were inclusive?
- What if we operated from abundance?
- What if we went bold?

Unfortunately, these three prompts are often in opposition to how we normally operate as a sector, but they are essential to solution brainstorming. And to be clear, when I say "solution" or "solving the problem," I'm not under the illusion that you will entirely address and/or eradicate a challenge (especially one that is intertwined and supported by oppressive systems and institutions), but you *can* truly make progress to change people's lives and reach powerful organizational outcomes.

**What if we were inclusive?** Most problem-solving is problematically completed by executive leaders and board members, and often in silos and restricted by hierarchies. In the social sector, we often do not provide inclusive, equitable access and shared power for internal and external stakeholders to fully participate in problem-solving.

Diversity is an essential piece of solution brainstorming and testing, and it connects to the value of diverse teams, diverse organizations, and diverse perspectives based on a wide variety of positionalities, biases, and experiences. Our sector is severely constricted by not including all stakeholders and their lived and living experiences to inform and drive our missions.

**What if we operated in abundance?** This prompt is so important because as a sector we are often trapped by (and rewarded for maintaining) our scarcity mindsets. I often joke that how we currently brainstorm is to say, "Okay, we've got five dollars, five minutes, and five people: What can we create?" That is not very inspiring and will generate pretty mundane and often disappointing potential solutions. You can do a lot with five people (due to the power of small and mighty teams), but you must think beyond time and money as you explore solutions and let testing take you where you need to go.

It is essential to brainstorm with a mindset of abundance. When we traditionally focus on building just *one* solution without testing, it raises the stakes, pressure, and resource investment so significantly that we feel we must "make the solution work."

**What if we were bold?** Often, we are limited by immediately thinking about technical feasibility, or how we might pull off an idea, but when we are trying to go bold, we want to be open to any and all possibilities. *What if instead of falling back into patterns of saying, "That would never work," you shift to considering how you might truly address the problems experienced by stakeholders? What if you went a step further and considered what it would look like to not only address a challenge, but also delight stakeholders?* I love imagining how to delight stakeholders, as so often we provide simplistic, band-aid, sympathetic, or "at least we tried" solutions. We want to codesign "knock your socks off," game-changing, and inspiring solutions.

## Solution Brainstorming

Solution brainstorming is usually people's favorite part of the PAUSE framework because it feels familiar and exciting. Most important is to keep your challenge (and any refinements you made to your challenge) and the key takeaways you gained from your interviews top of mind.

Before you jump into ideation mode and document every single idea that pops into your brilliant mind, I have one very important ground rule: There is to be no judgment or criticism of any idea that you (or your team) generate. This is time to consider, without limiting yourself or others, what could be possible. The more ideas, the better; some teams will generate more than forty potential solution ideas. This is not the time to limit your thinking and focus on practicality or feasibility.

There are so many people who stop themselves by evaluating each idea and thinking, "Leadership will never support this," or "We tried that before and it didn't work." Again, this is time for wide-open, unrestrained brainstorming. What I like to say is that when you're brainstorming, some of the ideas should make you laugh and saying some of them out loud might even make you feel embarrassed. That's great! I say to go as bold as possible and not worry about future implementation because through testing, you may arrive at extraordinary and unexpected solutions.

Let me share an inspiring example. I worked with a team that was brainstorming potential solutions for affordable early childcare, and one of the team members had an idea they were embarrassed to share because they thought it was beyond possibility. The idea was to provide childcare at employee worksites to make it really accessible to families and potentially create a new revenue stream for the organization. Luckily, that sticky note made it into the stack of possibilities, and through Solution Testing, they learned that partnering with businesses in their community to provide contracted on-site childcare *was* a viable option. In fact, they had so much early validation that they secured a $500,000 grant to establish their first site, and their idea was soon after recognized by an angel investment firm as a model they wanted to invest in and scale! You never know where the learning journey will take you, so I implore you to document everything you can think of.

So now that you are ready to be as creative and open-minded as possible, document as many potential solution ideas as you can, one idea per paper or virtual sticky note, answering the prompt, "What potential solution might address the stakeholder's problem?"

## Solution Prioritizing

After you are finished with your very thorough brain dump, organize your ideas in a slightly different way. Since you can't jump in and test every single idea, it is important to prioritize and choose a starting point. Once again, your goal is to be super focused and work efficiently and effectively.

One of my very favorite ways to get focused is by creating a two-by-two table. This will help you focus your efforts on those potential solutions that could really be the most helpful to stakeholders and generate a significant positive response. These are hypotheses that you will be able to test very soon!

**USE A 2 × 2 TO PRIORITIZE POTENTIAL SOLUTIONS**

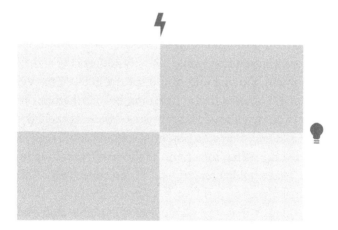

Take one paper or virtual sticky note that has one of your potential ideas (work with one potential solution idea at a time) and "slide" it along the horizontal x-axis (the one with the light bulb indicating what you hypothesize the stakeholder will think is a "bright" or "dim" idea). You are guessing the reaction stakeholders might have based on your interviews and knowledge (how you think they would perceive the idea and how much it stands out to them or not).

To find what space you think your sticky notes should occupy, consider whether this potential solution might make the stakeholder say, "Wow! This is great and I've been really wanting something like this!" (the "brighter" the idea, the farther on the right side of the x-axis), or if they might fall on the other end of the spectrum (on the left, "dimmer" side), where their response might be, "Meh, I guess that's okay," or "I've seen this before and it's . . . whatever." These might be slight exaggerations of real-life stakeholder reactions, but you get the point. You want to hypothesize where their reaction might fall on that x-axis, somewhere between "Whoa!" and "So what."

Now you need to hypothesize, based on your knowns and empathy interview learning, where you could put your sticky note on the y-axis. You want to consider how likely it is that your potential solution would actually address the stakeholder's problem. On one end of the spectrum is, "That would really help!" (closer to the lightning bolt, or higher on the y-axis)—you hypothesize that the stakeholder is excited, optimistic, and feels that your potential solution could really help them. On the other, lower end of the spectrum, they might think, "That wouldn't really help," "I don't want that," "I don't want to do that," or, just "No."

The idea is that you take every sticky note and glide it around the two-by-two table until you think you've found the right placement for each one. Your ultimate goal is to look at the sticky notes that end up in the upper right-hand quadrant (really positive reaction and really positive perception of potential impact) and pick one; that is the potential solution you will test first. So, what is the first potential solution that you want to test?

Not only does the two-by-two table help you prioritize, but it is also a visual record of all the ideas you (and your team) came up with, which you can go back to anytime. Let's say your first, second, or even third idea from that quadrant is a no-go; you still have an abundance of different ideas you can pursue. If you test an idea and realize it is not the best fit, that is not failure; it is amazing learning leading you closer to your next opportunity to create impact. The visual power of the solution prioritization two-by-two table is also very exciting to leaders and colleagues. They can see your creativity and recognize that in this process, when you're working with a challenge that has a lot of uncertainty, you need the fluidity and flexibility to learn.

### What This Activity Looks like with Your Team

When you are brainstorming potential solutions, team members should work individually and document as many potential solution ideas as they can. Then as each team member shares their ideas, one at a time, and as a group, you organize them on the two-by-two table. It's important at this stage that when you present and share your sticky notes as a team, no one provides lengthy descriptions of the potential solutions. In other words, no one should detail or pitch the structure, timeline, tasks required, and so on, of their solution. One might need to add clarity if the team is unclear about what an initial description means, but you are trying to keep it simple at this stage and complete the prioritization. You might need to lean on your team to get feedback on where sticky notes should be placed, but your ultimate goal as a team is still the same—to focus first on the solutions on the sticky notes in the upper right-hand quadrant (really positive reaction and really positive perception of potential impact). As a team, you will pick one potential solution that you want to work on testing.

## What Are You Assuming?

Now that you have chosen which potential solution you want to test first (very exciting!), I don't want you to just jump in and implement your idea; you first need to focus on uncovering additional uncertainty in the form of embedded assumptions. The next set of provocations for this skill include:

- What if we knew what would work before we built it?
- What if we reduced our risk?
- What if we could learn quickly and creatively?

This idea of knowing what will work before you build anything is super important, and it's not how we typically work. The PAUSE framework is different because it's really about using Solution Testing to get very clear data and signals of what you know is going to address your challenge. Working in these new ways reduces your risk significantly. You can find out if your project or program will actually create value before you design a plan, assign a team, create a website, craft paperwork, imagine activities, draft evaluation materials, or apply for a grant. The best part is that you gain this clarity and evidence in a matter of hours, weeks, or, at most, months, significantly reducing your risk of wasted time, energy, and resources.

In its current form, the sector is often anything but fast and nimble, "scrappy," or decisive. It would most likely be described as bureaucratic, slow, and stodgy. Because of our fears of risk and failure, we move slowly and in ways we think are methodical, "best practiced," and super cautious, but unfortunately, when we do this, we often unintentionally create weak impact and tremendous waste, at scale.

## "Breaking" Our Solutions

What I love most about Solution Testing is that we don't have to think of our solutions as precious— they're not "the only ones we've got" or "our only hope." We are working in abundance, and not only do we have a large set of options, but we are also following the learning journey that will continue to reveal opportunities! This way of thinking and working to "break" your potential solution might feel awkward and uncomfortable because it is antithetical to how we are taught to operate, but I hope you have seen so far the power of shifting your thinking and actions.

As a result of testing your potential solution, you will know the number of people who do and do not want, or are not able, to participate in your solution, and by using your awesome empathy skills, you're able to understand why this is the case. Again, we don't purchase everything we could buy, and not everyone will participate in your solution, for many different reasons. Solution Testing is all about addressing this more deeply. You are trying to see if your potential solution is valuable enough that stakeholders will take action, can take action, invest their own resources to participate, and potentially benefit. You then can go deeper to understand why a solution was or was not embraced and continue the process of codesigning and testing other potential solutions.

The other very powerful aspect of Solution Testing is that it gives you the ability to share what you're learning and how it is informing your decisions, and, in turn, how it can shape the decisions of your leaders. A leader will almost never ignore the information a staff member or team imparts after having interviewed many stakeholders and after running a handful of tests that resulted in very clear insights about next steps. I love this feedback that one of my clients once shared:

"Solution Testing provides a really nice way to tell your boss that their idea sucks." We have to admit that sometimes *all* of our ideas stink. Solution Testing empowers individuals and teams to say something more polite and evidence-informed such as, "Your idea sounded so promising and we thought it could help our stakeholders, but you know what? We talked to a lot of people and we ran many tests, and it turns out that nobody wanted that solution." It's a bonus if you can add extra value by sharing something like, "We actually learned that the real challenge is X," or "The stakeholder really needs Y," or "Actually, Z is the very best solution." Even the most dogmatic, command-and-control, closed-minded leaders have a very hard time fighting back against the data because they often have not talked to a single stakeholder, and they have not run any tests. Leaders will usually rely on the excellent work of their staff and teams and listen to their recommendations.

What I also enjoy about Solution Testing is that there is a mechanism and process for sharing learning. There are no closed doors and no solutions created in silos and vacuums. There are "witnesses," multiple layers of staff and stakeholders who are often engaged, and usually other leaders and staff in the organization who are watching the learning and hearing the feedback. This also increases the level of buy-in from leaders because if they were to completely ignore the learning or go with some other untested idea, it would create extreme dissonance and potential concern. In other words, leaders are highly motivated to pay attention and listen to your (and your team's) suggestions.

## Identifying and Prioritizing Your Assumptions

Because you've spent time identifying your positionalities, naming your unknowns, preparing for and, hopefully, being touched and changed by your empathy interviews, plus brainstorming abundantly, you are now perfectly poised to consider your assumptions. American actor Alan Alda once said, "Your assumptions are your windows on the world. Scrub them off every once in a while or the light won't come in." Just as we need to pause and consider all of the uncertainties and tensions we hold in this work, we have to recognize, name, and prioritize all of the embedded assumptions we take for granted.

Assumptions underlie every single solution. Assumptions are what we think is true without question; we feel sure we know something, but often without data to really back it up. Do you recall how when I asked you to think of your challenge, the stakeholder, and how the stakeholder might talk about the challenge in their own words, I called those hypotheses? That's because it was early in the process and there was (and still are) an abundance of assumptions to be uncovered. Some of the phrases that raise the hairs on the back of my neck and alert me to assumptions are when people say things like, "Of course they will...," "I know that...," or "I am sure that..." These are signs that someone might be making an assumption. This is usually especially true when someone's referring to a stakeholder group they are not a part of.

When we think about assumptions, we want to situate them in the context of all the actions we are assuming stakeholders will take in order to access, participate in, and benefit from our solution. For this next activity, you will brainstorm assumptions around the prompt, "What must be true for the stakeholder to derive benefit from the potential solution?" When you brainstorm assumptions, you want to stay super focused on what *stakeholders* need to do in order to experience value, not on what *you* need to do, so we write each assumption as, "Stakeholders will..."

An example might help add clarity. Remember the team who wanted to explore ways in which they could increase the recruitment and retention of caregivers in their early childhood home visitation program? They recognized that sitting at a folding table for several hours with displays of brochures and some cute giveaways usually generated only a handful of names of interested caregivers on their clipboard. The major "aha" moment they generated from interviewing past or lapsed and current caregivers in their program was that the organization was expecting caregivers to *imagine* the impact of their programs just by looking at a brochure, table display, and/or website.

The team brainstormed different ways they could reach caregivers in their more natural, day-to-day environments in the community, and one of their potential solutions was to get out from "behind the table" and reach their stakeholders in public places, like the grocery store, to engage them and their children in hands-on activities. Their rationale was that if they could reach caregivers and provide immediate value and benefit using an engaging activity, then more caregivers would be motivated to sign up to learn more and potentially register for resources.

Some assumptions embedded in this new outreach idea were:

- Stakeholders will want to be approached at the grocery store.
- Stakeholders will have time to talk to us.
- Stakeholders will want to talk to us.
- Stakeholders will complete the activity.

- Stakeholders will give us feedback.
- Stakeholders will like the activity.
- Stakeholders will want additional information.
- Stakeholders will sign up for programs.

Rather than pausing to identify assumptions, status quo problem-solving might include a leader choosing the idea for a new outreach strategy and putting it into practice. Instead, we want to begin testing the assumptions that are built into the potential solution, rather than building out the full solution. You might notice that some assumptions must come earlier than others—for example, "Stakeholders will want to talk to us" would come before "Stakeholders will want additional information." As you test earlier assumptions, you can rule out or uncover information that will be helpful in addressing assumptions that might come later or that are connected.

Before you begin to brainstorm assumptions embedded in your potential solution, I want to mention that we rarely identify the latent assumptions in our collaborative work (let alone test-drive potential collaborations before we put them into action). This may be partly due to the often rushed way we get letters of support or how organizations are at times mandated to work together, but more often than not, it's due to the lack of mechanisms and skills to test the "say versus do" assumptions embedded within collective work. Unfortunately, untested assumptions can be lethal to collaboration. In this case, assumptions are all the things that must be true for the collaboration to be successful, and these usually sound something like, "Of course, partners will: refer clients to our program, advertise our services, attend a majority of partnership meetings, share data, contribute to shared grant applications, provide staff or volunteers to support the program, provide space for programming, share financial resources," and so on. As you can see, some of these are pretty critical to success, so it is key to use the PAUSE skills, including Solution Testing, in your partnership work.

Okay, now it's time to identify assumptions embedded in your potential solution. Using sticky notes, brainstorm and document as many assumptions (one per sticky note) as possible answering the prompt, "What must be true for the stakeholder to derive benefit from the potential solution?" Remember to start each note with "Stakeholders will..."

### USE A 2 × 2 TO PRIORITIZE POTENTIAL ASSUMPTIONS

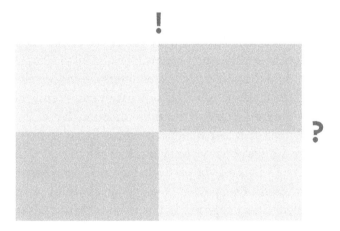

Similar to when you prioritized your potential solutions, you will now prioritize your assumptions. You cannot test every assumption at once, so you want to get a sense of which assumptions are the most important and unknown to the potential success of your solution. You will do a task similar to what you did before: "slide" your sticky note on a paper or virtual two-by-two along the two axes. Again, these are hypotheses, your best guesses, but the intent is to determine your next steps.

The x-axis is focused on the degree of uncertainty or how much you really know or understand about the assumption. On the right side of the x-axis, you see a question mark to signify how much clarity you really have about that assumption. The further you move your sticky note to the right, the more uncertain you are. Maybe you lack data on or past experience with this assumption and you have more to learn. On the other side of the spectrum, left on the x-axis, you place sticky notes that you feel pretty confident and certain about, possibly because you have clear experience, data, and knowledge related to this specific assumption.

On the y-axis, you are focusing on how important the assumption is to the solution creating potential benefit. The top of the y-axis (closer to the exclamation point) indicates that this is a very important assumption. Think of it as meaning "if this is not true, then the whole solution falls apart." On the other end of the spectrum, the bottom of the y-axis, you place the assumptions that are less important. These are assumptions that may not be deal breakers but still exist and deserve to be captured.

Once all of the sticky notes have been prioritized, focus on those that are most unsure and most important to the solution creating value, and choose one to start with from the upper right-hand quadrant. The one you choose is often referred to as the "riskiest assumption" and is yet another hypothesis that you will test to determine how to create the most value for stakeholders. So what do you think is the most uncertain and most important assumption that you want to test first?

Similar to the visual impact of the solution prioritization table, placing your many assumptions into quadrants is a powerful way to get your colleagues and leaders to also understand the significant number of assumptions embedded in the challenge, and probably in other existing work as well. The prioritization two-by-two table also keeps all of your assumptions organized so that as you run your solution tests, you can continue to return to the upper right-hand quadrant of assumptions until you have the validation that you are ready (or not) to move toward implementation.

### What This Activity Looks like with Your Team

After each team member takes time to identify assumptions individually, the team will rejoin and use the two-by-two table to prioritize their collective assumptions. One team member at a time will share their sticky notes and, with team feedback, begin to place them in the appropriate quadrants. Remember to place similar or identical sticky notes near or right on top of identical notes to move them into groups.

## PAUSE AND CONSIDER

**YOU HAVE** now practiced a whole new way to brainstorm! Woohoo! Most of us are already pretty good at coming up with ideas because it connects to our natural skills and status quo problem-solving tendencies. I hope you see that by embracing inclusion, abundance, and bold thinking, you can exceed your previous expectations of what's possible. By not just randomly picking what sounds best or easiest, or a pet project, you prioritized what you thought would be the most exciting to stakeholders and the most impactful potential solution, and you are now set up for the next step of the process, which is putting that potential solution to the test! Can you tell that I get excited about this phase?

When I talked about trying to "break" your solution, it might have felt jarring, or maybe a bit intriguing. We normally don't want to jeopardize our solutions; we want to protect, nurture, and grow them (after all, we are putting in a lot of work to make them possible). One of the most common outcomes—and one of my favorites—of people using the PAUSE framework is that they begin to see assumptions all through their work. They notice when a debate of ideas is actually a debate about different assumptions and hypotheses that need to be tested; they see how other existing programs and processes were unintentionally built on shaky foundations of assumptions; and as their self-awareness builds, they begin to notice when they are assuming something must be true without the data to back it up. Most people actually like having this new superpower, especially because they also know how to test those assumptions. Consider these questions:

- Think of the last time you brainstormed a potential solution. What challenge were you trying to address? How many ideas did you come up with? Did you come up with ideas on your own? Did you consult with colleagues?

- How are ideas generated in your organization? Who brainstorms ideas?

- How would you rate your personal level of boldness in terms of bold thinking? How about your organization and leadership?

- How did it feel to brainstorm without judgment? Is self-criticism typically a problem for you? How does judging the ideas of others show up for you and in your organization?

- How did it feel to prioritize your ideas? How do you feel about the idea you've selected for testing? Any hesitancy, excitement, fear?

- How did it feel to identify assumptions embedded within your potential solution? What was your favorite part of the exercise? Least favorite part?

- How did it feel to prioritize your assumptions, and what do you think of the most uncertain and most important assumption you selected?

# 13

# Designing Your
# Solution Test

I T'S A hard pill to swallow that even if a potential solution
is super exciting to *you*, logically makes sense, is bold, *and*
seems like it will satisfy stakeholders' greatest needs, the
wheels can still fall off when your solution gets in front of a
group of stakeholders. While that can be discouraging for sure,
your goal is to gather learning as quickly as possible so that you
can rapidly and efficiently guide your decision-making.

And as with your empathy questions, it is less helpful to
ask someone what they think they will do than ask about what
they have actually done. The same is true for gaining feedback and testing your potential solution. It is very tempting
to share your solution idea and ask a stakeholder if they like
it or would use it, and then accept that answer as evidence
to guide your next steps. People truly mean well, but there is
often a "say versus do" disconnect, and there's so much that
can happen between thought and reality. Many times, I have
seen stakeholders say, "That looks good," or "That could be
helpful," but when the team returns to see if they *will actually use* the solution, the stakeholders then say, "I thought it

was great for someone else," "I don't need that," or "I actually wouldn't use that." While this unexpected feedback can shape a helpful learning moment, you can save time and energy by setting up a strong solution test that is based on *behavior*.

I mentioned this in the previous chapter, but it bears repeating: To test your solution, you are not building out the full solution and then sharing that with stakeholders (since that could be a potential waste of resources). Instead, you are testing the assumptions embedded within the potential solution related to the actions people must take. We often think that to interact with stakeholders, we have to have something "perfect" or fully built out to show them. This is not true.

Your focus at this stage is to learn if and how people might access, use, and benefit from your solution by seeing what they are willing and able to do to invest their precious time, energy, and resources. You are using your creative juices to determine how you can create value from a solution that does not yet exist, and you are essentially creating a first draft or a prototype to test assumptions.

All that said, since you are creating and testing a prototype of a solution, you should always be transparent with stakeholders about being in the early exploration stages of your learning journey. You will also once again secure consent from any stakeholder before engaging them in a solution test and sharing complete information about who you are, your goals, what will happen, and their rights and power, similar to the process you used before you conducted empathy interviews. As part of your test design, you should also plan for how you will create some initial value for the stakeholder. For example, in the case of the early childhood home visitation program trying to gain greater student enrollment and retention, the team approached caregivers in the grocery store and gave them a children's book and brochure about existing programs. You always want to have something you can offer people, and it can include elements such as compensation, incentives, and resources.

Because in most cases your solution does not yet exist and you are approaching a stakeholder who might have a real need for resources, you need to also make sure that you are equipped to connect them to existing resources at that moment of engagement. You never want a stakeholder to engage, be vulnerable, and provide benefit to you and then walk away feeling as if there was no value exchange or support available.

Designing a solution test is actually pretty simple, but it can still be one of the most intimidating parts of this work. I think it feels overwhelming because there are so many different tests you could potentially design for each assumption, which is actually very good because you have many options for learning.

I like to keep it very simple, so I use a fill-in-the-blank-style prompt. "If we _____ [make some 'offer'], we expect stakeholders will _____ [the behavior you'd like to see]." You are really just constructing another hypothesis statement to test.

Those two blanks include two areas to consider. The first, "make some 'offer,'" is about how you are going to engage stakeholders so they interact with your potential solution. How will you find stakeholders? What will you say to them? What will you show them? The other half of this fill-in-the-blank statement is what "behavior you'd like to see" from stakeholders. Once you make your "offer," what do you anticipate, want, or need people to do to indicate they might access, use, and benefit from your solution? Do they have to show up to do something? Do they have to interact with something and share feedback? Do they have to provide information? Do they have to sign up for something?

Let's start with a theoretical hypothesis statement using our caregiver outreach example. The team wanted to conduct their solution test at a grocery store because they knew that many caregivers with young children often struggle while shopping with little ones. The team wanted to design an interactive game that would create an immediate impact on caregivers and their kids, so they created a grocery store bingo activity in just fifteen minutes. It was very sweet and included prompts in the different squares such as "find something with the color yellow," and "find the letter 'W.'"

Here is the fill-in-the-blank statement again: "If we _____ [make some 'offer'], we expect the stakeholder will _____ [the behavior you'd like to see]." For our example, that statement would become, "If we approach caregivers in a grocery store and ask them to play grocery store bingo with their child, stakeholders [in this case, caregivers] will complete the activity and give us positive feedback."

I will share the results of their test as well as additional examples of a variety of solution tests, but first, it is your turn to craft your solution test hypothesis. Think of your hypothesis as documentation of what you *want* to happen, or the best-case scenario. When you launch the test and collect all of your very important quantitative and qualitative data, you will compare them to this statement to see how well it matches (or doesn't).

So, what is your solution test? "If we _____ [make some 'offer'], we expect the stakeholder will _____ [the behavior you'd like to see]."

Now that you have designed your first solution test, there are a few caveats to also consider to optimize your learning.

**Remember how empathy is never "done"?** Solution tests are a perfect time to use your growing empathy skills. You are collecting data and also trying to understand people's behaviors.

For the caregiver example, the team had not only the grocery store bingo activity but also some very brief questions to help them learn whether or not the activity was beneficial and why. They also asked parents to leave their contact details if they were interested in receiving additional information. You never just want to take the results of a solution test at face value and, if possible, you want to use the opportunity to connect with stakeholders to gain additional learning.

If time permits, it is super helpful to also ask additional questions that are connected to other unknowns and assumptions. For example, since the early childhood home visitation program team was approaching new stakeholders, upon consent they could have asked their previously crafted empathy interview questions and/or perhaps asked new questions they created after their initial interviews revealed additional areas of uncertainty.

**Is the behavior you'd like to see easily achievable?** This might sound odd because we want stakeholders to be easily able to access, use, and benefit from our potential solutions, but sometimes when we provide an offer, the behavior we want to see can be pretty easy to satisfy. As a result, we are still left with a lower degree of confidence that this solution will really create the most value. To gather results that will give you a stronger level of data and confidence, you want to increase the level of engagement.

In the garden example I shared earlier, the board member emailed her friends and asked if they wanted to be involved and become garden volunteers. It is pretty simple to hit reply and say, "Sure, sign me up!" When she asked those same interested people to then attend a meeting in person in order to choose their volunteer assignment, that list of about eighty people who had emailed "Yes!" dwindled to three. This is an example of increasing the "investment" required of

stakeholders to see if a potential solution is important or helpful to them. To double-check that your test is constructed to
generate helpful results, pause and ask yourself, "Does this
test I'm designing really help me learn more about the key
assumption?" and "Will the way I've structured the test generate information that will help me make decisions moving
forward?"

**You should be in data collection mode.** Your goal is to collect
as much quantitative and qualitative data as possible from
your solution test. You want to count the number of interactions with stakeholders and the "offers" that were accepted
and denied. Make note of what you observe from body language (again, taking cultural factors into consideration) and
the information you gain during your additional empathy
interviews, plus any ideas, questions, or unknowns that pop up.

For the grocery store bingo test, the team not only made
note of how they successfully got approval from the store
manager to conduct their test, but also tracked every person
they approached and made separate tick marks for those who
agreed to talk to them, those who took the activity, those who
completed the activity, and those who provided their contact information. They also had detailed notes of caregivers'
feedback about whether they liked the activity, as well as the
knowledge they gained from asking extra empathy questions.

**Return for more feedback.** Don't forget that when you prepare
to run your test and are deciding on whom you will contact, in
many cases, you have a lovely set of very kind individuals who
have already talked to you for your empathy interviews. You
might feel shy or nervous about going back to the same stakeholders you interviewed, but if they provided permission for
you to return, they are usually pretty excited when you actually

come back, and most people still want to be helpful. Of course, continue to gain consent, act with humility, empathy, respect, and gratitude for your amazingly helpful stakeholders, and provide additional compensation.

You might also have a list of individuals whom stakeholders recommended you also talk to (a tip about asking for recommendations of who else to contact is just one I include in a list of must-have interview questions on my book website, NoMoreStatusQuoBook.com), so perhaps if you did not get to include them in the initial empathy interview stage, you could reach out to those stakeholders at this point. If you need to reach out to a new set of stakeholders, just be focused on specifically whom you are trying to create value for and what you learned from your previous empathy interviews.

Some tests can also involve "strangers," such as the grocery shoppers in the early childhood example. As applicable, of course, to the stakeholder, potential solution, and test design, you can find stakeholders who are new to you at public events, online, or via email lists.

As you can see, just as assumptions are very specific to your potential solution, solution tests are also very specific to the assumption you are testing. Teams usually can design most tests in less than thirty minutes and some tests can be run in less than an hour, while others may require more time. It just depends on the assumption, the test design, and your creativity. In the next chapter focused on the final skill of the PAUSE framework, Evidence-Informed Decision-Making, you will learn how to make choices about your next steps based on all you learn from your solution test results.

## Solution Test Storytime

Because Solution Testing can feel overwhelming and is so dependent on what you need to test, I want to share a very small sample of actual tests designed by teams, and the results they gathered. I hope that these stories inspire you and increase your confidence in designing and conducting solution tests.

### Should We Buy This Software?

I was working with a local government and they were concerned that people who were coming to their permit department to secure permits for projects (like adding a fence to a property or doing a home renovation) were frustrated with the process, which required a trip to city hall. They were looking into new software, at an expense of about $150,000, that would enable people to complete and submit permit paperwork online instead of coming downtown. The idea sounded innovative, more efficient, and time-saving. But it was a risky assumption that people wanted to fill out the paperwork electronically rather than use the standard triplicate paper form. To conduct the solution test, we trained the staff member at the reception desk to ask people if they would like to fill out the traditional paper form or fill out the electronic version using a tablet. To create the latter, we simply made a Google form and typed the first ten questions of the triplicate form, so that it looked semi-professional. Luckily, the department office was surrounded by glass like a large fishbowl, so we were able to sit and watch what happened.

As we watched the busy permit desk for nearly an hour, not a single person chose the electronic version. In fact, not one person wanted to touch the tablet. As people exited the department, we asked if we could have a moment of their time in order to understand why they had chosen paper over the digital option. Overwhelmingly, stakeholders shared that they were not tech-savvy and did not feel comfortable using computer technology. Most of them also did not have an administrator or someone at their office who handled technology, so, if possible, they avoided it altogether. They also shared that they enjoyed coming to city hall because out of all of the local area cities, this was the speediest in the region. They also enjoyed coming in person because while they were physically present, it usually reminded them of other tasks they needed to complete with other departments, and as an added bonus, they usually ran into friends and colleagues, so it was a space for professional and personal connection. When the team took the results back to the decision-makers, they were surprised by the results. Leaders were delighted that their city was seen as providing quality services and that stakeholders were satisfied (something they assumed was not the case), and they decided not to purchase the software and to explore ways that those funds could be used elsewhere.

## How Can We Support More Families?

The grocery store bingo test team thought of another strategy to potentially create immediate value for caregivers, which included a similar risky assumption—that people would be attracted by a new approach to potentially generate more interest in their programs. Since the team's goal was to "get out from behind the table" at community events, at one information fair, they spread out a large blanket in front of the table and displayed a big binder full of colorful pictures of different toys that can be made using standard recyclable items. They also had a box of recyclables on the blanket and invited families to make a toy. Caregivers and children were drawn to their area and were very interested in both playing and learning more about what the organization was offering. Instead of the staff practically begging people to talk to them, caregivers were asking, "Who are you and what other cool stuff do you offer?" This reinforced what the team had learned in their initial empathy interviews—that it was difficult for caregivers to imagine services and benefits, and that experiencing samples of activities and seeing results firsthand make a significant difference.

### Can We Do This Together?

You can also use solution tests to try out and better understand collaborative partnerships. I worked with an organization that wanted to align efforts with other agencies in their same space to advocate for a citywide policy change that would positively impact community members. Before spearheading this large initiative, they wanted to see beyond "promises of support" from partners because this effort would be a significant undertaking. Specifically, they knew that to get started they needed to collect data from each partner agency about the current state of affairs in their city.

Their key assumptions included:

- The stakeholder will have the data we need.

- The stakeholder will have permission to share their data.

- The stakeholder will know how to access and package the data to be shared.

- The stakeholder will share their data.

Their riskiest assumption was that these partners would be willing to share their data. They knew that program data was sensitive and that having united data from across multiple organizations would be key to potentially shaping the policy and outreach efforts. Their solution test included sharing their vision with community partners and asking for a few very specific pieces of data. They wanted to see if they would actually be given the data, which as you can see, was connected to several other key assumptions.

Fortunately, they were able to demonstrate that, in fact, these partners were committed to joining forces, and most importantly, they realized that different partners had different needs, obstacles, and abilities related to data. Some partners readily provided data and others were committed but experienced challenges like software limitations. The team learned that while their partners were overall committed to the shared mission, to be ultimately successful, their efforts would need to be highly customized, and they would need to accommodate and support each partner's data capabilities.

## How Do We Find Information in Our Organization?

One of my favorite tests was conducted by an organization that was seeing a breakdown in internal referrals from staff. This is a giant agency that serves a large community and has many different physical sites. Staff at individual sites knew what resources they had to offer and had their go-to personal resource guide and favorite colleagues to contact, but the concern was that many did not know about the breadth and depth of other resources that were offered in other locations or by the organization overall. The fear was that this lack of knowledge not only could limit the potential to successfully connect community members to resources but also might be an indicator of a significant need for internal training and enhanced communication pathways.

The team designed and conducted a secret shopper–style test: They had one of their volunteers who was on the team pose as a community member and contact multiple sites asking for resources for a very specific need. The team then monitored the response time and how those requests were forwarded in the organization. The risky assumption was that the staff would be able to get the referral to the right contact.

Unfortunately, after contact with several different sites and several attempts, not a single person was able to connect this "decoy" community member with the necessary resources. The leadership had an idea that internal disconnects might be rippling out to impact their external stakeholders, but it was very difficult and eye-opening to watch it play out in real time. As a result of this confirmation, the organization created an interactive resource search tool that would show local office and organization-wide resources, and they instituted meet-and-greet activities so that staff across different sites could make trusted connections and share about their various programs.

THIS IS just a very small selection of stories that illustrate the power of Solution Testing. Based on the organization, challenge, stakeholder, potential solution, key assumptions, and your ingenuity (and that of your team), there are many different tests that can be designed.

## PAUSE AND CONSIDER

**SOLUTION TESTING** is one of the most powerful skills you can use and develop when you are trying to address a challenge. What I find most empowering is that you have a way to find answers about what you should do next. Reducing uncertainty and choosing a path forward (that is informed by evidence) feels good because it releases that soothing dopamine, and it feels doubly good because you are seeing true *action*.

I acknowledge that designing a solution test can feel hard or confusing. Most people want to ensure they're "doing it right." The key to quality tests is being thoughtful; it is pausing to consider what you need to learn, how you will reach your very generous stakeholders, what you will offer, and what you will measure. Solution tests are a rich source of information and learning of all kinds, so the answer is that tests don't have to be perfect; you just have to get started. Consider these questions:

- How did it feel to design a test based on your riskiest assumption?

- What are you most excited about when you think about designing and conducting a solution test? What about it makes you most concerned?

- Were the examples of solution tests helpful? Were there any examples that resonated most or that sparked inspiration?

**14**

# Evidence-Informed Decision-Making

THIS IS the final skill of the PAUSE framework and it is all about how you and your organization can most quickly and effectively make decisions. There are three provocations for this skill:

- What if success = learning?
- What if we had clarity on why something worked (or didn't)?
- What if we could guide decision-making with evidence?

In the social sector, we usually define program deliverables as our metrics of success, but what if *learning* could also be our metric of success? What if we could share what worked or didn't without retribution, take "risks," and share learning in our organizations and across the sector? I truly believe that if you adopt a learning mindset, no matter the results, there is no failure when you are addressing uncertainty. All results spell success, positive *and* negative, because they allow you to make informed decisions.

Unfortunately, because we are so failure-averse and fearful of consequences, we often hide when something does not work. Missteps or ineffective programs are often just swept under the rug and kept private, especially from donors and funders. As a sector, we say we want leading-edge and innovative change, but we fear anything new or untested, and bold ideas are often seen as risky opportunities. What is interesting is that many organizations are creating programs every day without stakeholder input and testing, and *that* is truly the biggest risk and is generating tremendous waste and weak impact at scale.

That said, I've even heard funders share that many of the programs they fund do not create impact and some of them behave as if they're fine with those results. This illuminates not only the power and accountability disconnect around metrics in the sector but also an enormous missed opportunity to understand and share why programs were ineffective.

Because organizations usually have no mechanisms through which to share learning, we often know very little about why programs don't work. We just notice that a program disappeared or was shuttered, the funding ended, and the staff were let go. There is very rarely any analysis or sharing of lessons learned.

Sometimes another, more frustrating reality plagues our organizations: services, programs, and processes that we *know* don't work become institutionalized and continue unchecked. The same is true for programs that linger in the murky middle; they do not have obvious signs of failure, but it is unclear if they really work or how they create value, so they continue as well.

Decisions to end or keep a program should not be made without evidence. We need to understand *why* a program is not providing a viable or impactful solution and be able to communicate that to decision-makers (and hopefully explore alternative options). Conversely, we also want to know why a program is really fantastic and how it creates positive impact so we can increase buy-in and investment, and potentially optimize and scale that work.

Another benefit of making decisions based on evidence is that power is more equitably distributed. Evidence limits the adoption of pet projects and holds leaders and others accountable for proving that what *they* think will be really great will actually create value for stakeholders. Most leaders are doing the best they can to make decisions and meet the expectation that they have all the answers, but guiding leaders and providing them with evidence and justification based on what you have learned can be very powerful and helpful in shifting your organization and outcomes.

The power of the PAUSE framework is that there is a process, a shared language, and steps you can take to clearly understand why stakeholders do and do not engage. The results of your tests give you the evidence you need to decide if you should build something (or not) *before* you invest extensive time and resources. You generate data and know the reasons *why* a proposed solution will and won't create value.

## Collecting Evidence

Once you've run your solution test, you need to document everything you have learned—your quantitative data to produce numerical results and the qualitative data of your observations and key learning. You will document key takeaways, one per sticky note, and these takeaways should be grouped into themes.

You will produce a summary of your learning that—using the grocery store bingo example—might looking something like this:

- The team approached twenty caregivers on this date, at this time, at X grocery store.

- Fifteen of the twenty caregivers we approached talked to us and took the activity (those who said no shared that they were in a hurry and did not have time).

- Fourteen out of the fifteen caregivers who took the activity completed it with their child and returned to us to share feedback.

- All fourteen said that they and their child both enjoyed the activity (they shared feedback such as, "I never knew they knew that," "That was really fun," and "They were so well-behaved").

- The most frequent questions we heard were, "What group are you with again?" "Do you have more activities like this?"

- Ten of the fourteen caregivers provided their contact information to learn more.

- People really appreciated the book and brochure as a thank you.

So, thinking about the assumptions the team was testing, looking at this data, and considering the solution test hypothesis—"If we approach caregivers in a grocery store and ask them to play grocery store bingo with their child, stakeholders [in this case, caregivers] will complete the activity and give us positive feedback"—how do you think the team did?

I would feel comfortable saying that the team validated their hypothesis and got a result that matched what they hoped would happen. A large portion of caregivers they connected with were willing to share their time, and the activity got a positive response and even resulted in inquiries and interest in the organization and its services.

While this is exciting, before moving on, it was very important that they pause to think about and hypothesize why they got those results and then document those insights and guesses. For example, the data shows that they had a successful time approaching caregivers. Did their outreach strategy work because they first engaged the child by showing *them* the activity? Did the team have a very outgoing staff member who was really great at talking to strangers? Did the book incentive really seem to catch people's eye? These observations are helpful learning and key to shaping eventual solutions.

Now let's say that the team had a different set of data points.

- The team approached twenty caregivers on this date, at this time, at X grocery store.

- Five of the twenty caregivers we approached talked to us and took the activity (those who did not either ignored the offer or shared that they were in a hurry and did not have time).

- Two of the five caregivers who took the activity completed it with their child and returned to us to share feedback.

- Both caregivers said that the activity was "interesting," but neither had time to answer the additional questions, and neither provided their contact information to learn more.

- The two caregivers appreciated the book and brochure as a thank you.

As you can see, this data tells a very different story. Looking at these data points, it seems as though it was hard to even connect with caregivers, and few of those who did take the activity completed it. Those who did were not very effusive.

While these are very different results from the other data set, they are still successful and very helpful in informing your decision-making.

Even with tests that give you fewer or different results than what you hoped to see, it is still key to make sure that you pause to question why you think you got the results you did. What was going on? Were there factors connected to stakeholders or to the team to consider? For stakeholders, maybe the grocery store was too busy for connecting with people, or it was nap time and caregivers were in a hurry to get home, or maybe because it's odd to get stopped at the store, and it turned people off. The team might think that their results were lackluster due to something they did: maybe where they were standing was hard to notice, maybe they forgot to show the book as an incentive, or maybe the staff were less engaging and more passive. This analysis is very helpful when you are making your decision about your next steps.

So, what quantitative and qualitative data and key takeaways did you gather? Do you have ideas or hypotheses for why you got the data you did?

## Making a Decision

Once you run your test and create a summary of your quantitative and qualitative data, as well as any related insights into why you might have gotten the results you did, it is now time to decide what you will do with those results. There are three decisions to choose from: iterate, pivot, or persevere.

**When you choose to iterate,** you are considering, "How might I need to tweak this test and run it again?" When you choose to iterate, it means that you think your test design was pretty strong, but there's something about how the test was conducted that needs to be revised. For example, in the second data set, let's say the team believes that they got weak results due to nap time and being positioned in a hard-to-notice location in the grocery store. The team could choose to return to the store another day and time and set up in a different location, and try the test again.

**When you choose to pivot,** you are considering, "What about my challenge, stakeholder, or solution might be off?" The data and/or insights you gathered make a very clear suggestion that your solution is not viable or something that people want. This is different from when you choose to iterate, as there isn't an indication that something about the test design is off and needs to be retested; here, you have a clear indication that this is not a viable solution.

Pivoting can be hard but also creates powerful wake-up moments. You have to pause and appreciate (and, I would even add, celebrate!) the rapid and early learning, and consider if you need to rethink your challenge, re-engage with the same or different stakeholders, or go back to your solution prioritization two-by-two table and see what in the upper right-hand quadrant is the next best solution to test.

**When you choose to persevere,** you are considering, "What is the next assumption I need to test?" When you choose to persevere, it means that you are on the right track, but—before you get too excited—it also means that you validated only one (or just a few) of the many assumptions you need to test before you move to execution.

You should go back to your two-by-two assumption prioritization table and choose another risky assumption from the upper right-hand quadrant. You will then design and run a test for that assumption to gather additional results. Once the solution has been validated by multiple assumption tests, you can begin to examine which other stakeholders might benefit from the same potential solution or one that is adjusted to meet their needs.

I don't want to keep you in suspense, so I'll let you in on what really happened with the grocery store bingo team. When they ran their test, the team (who actually named themselves "Sausage Bits," inspired by the free samples of food sometimes offered at stores) received a lot of validation similar to the first sample data set. They chose to persevere (and at the same time sort of iterate) and try other public spaces where they thought they might find caregivers and children. The next place they went to was Peter Piper Pizza during lunch. They excitedly showed up to offer a similar activity, but found no families—most of the diners were adult business professionals! They were very surprised by this finding, and after a repeat attempt on a weekend, full of chaotic birthday parties, the pizza location was taken off their list. The next place they tried was a Chick-fil-A, and while the location was filled with families, it was challenging because kids were back and forth from the playground to the table, so it also was not ideal. The team talked about other options such as laundromats to continue these similar tests, and they ran their next solution test, during which they contacted people who had provided their information to see if they wanted to attend future workshops.

As you can see by the different paths they took, it is very important to document every step of your learning journey, including every unknown, question asked, insight gained, solution identified, assumption tested, and result collected. It is super powerful to demonstrate the winding path that you took chronologically, as every step with all its learning leads to the next. It is so difficult to recall over time all the ways you followed the learning, so it is essential to track it along the way.

After each test, you will follow the same pattern of deciding if you will iterate, pivot, or persevere. Once you have made your choice, plan your next steps based on that decision. You might tweak and rerun a test, go back to the drawing board to analyze where you might need to shift, or you might excitedly plan your next solution test based on your next key assumption. As you can see, these are not tests intended to be randomized controlled trials or to generate statistically significant results. These quick tests are meant to signal whether or not you are on the right path.

### What This Activity Looks like with Your Team

You will have designed and conducted your test as a team, divvying up tasks and roles. After the test, your team will work together to discuss and document everything you collectively learned. You will combine your quantitative data to produce numerical results. For the qualitative data—your observations and key learning—each team member will document those takeaways, one per sticky note, and share them with the team. Then you can all group similar takeaways into themes.

So, what decision did you make based on your data and insights? What are your next steps?

## PAUSE AND CONSIDER

**IT IS** super scary to think about failing. We feel fearful and uncertain about future consequences, and sometimes we feel powerless to control or prevent "failure" from happening. We have been trained not to fail and especially not to share our failures. *It is status quo thinking and problem-solving that has made failure the "F-word." To learn is to fail, and learning helps us reach success later.*

You can reframe "failure" and adopt new practices and decision-making skills that mitigate risk and help you learn and respond quickly. You can move on from a solution that turns out to be a dud, and if your solution seems to be a good possibility, you can feel clear and confident that you are making choices based on evidence and insights that have been validated by stakeholders. It's a pretty exhilarating feeling to know that what you are investing your resources in will actually create value. Consider these questions:

- What evidence do you typically collect about your work and its effectiveness? Do you use quantitative and qualitative data?

- Do you build programs based on early evidence of their potential effectiveness? How do you make decisions about the next steps to pursue when exploring or building a solution?

- Consider these three common categories of murky program effectiveness: 1) program disappeared but I don't know why, 2) program exists but the impact is unclear, and 3) program creates impact but the exact mechanisms for success are unknown. Can you think of programs in your organization that fall under any of these categories?

- Have you ever been asked to build a solution you did not feel confident would create a positive impact?

- Which of these three options, iterate, pivot, and persevere, would you say you most see in your work?

- If you ran your solution test and made a decision, how did it feel to make a choice?

# 15

# What to Do with Your Learning

HARE IT, share it, share it! One of the things I love about the PAUSE framework is that it's not only about learning but also about how to *share learning*. When I work with teams, it usually takes the form of multiday interactive workshops, in person or virtual, followed by twelve weeks of coaching. At the end of the final training day, teams give ten-minute presentations that summarize their entire experience and all they've learned in those past few days. This brief sharing style is very necessary these days: people, including and sometimes especially leaders, have a very short attention span, and learning needs to be shared in very direct bullet points using a clear outline people can follow again and again. Teams learn how to share what they've learned quickly and effectively with their teammates, leaders, and across the organization (and hopefully with all of their internal and external stakeholders as well).

*Share your learning with decision-makers in order to influence their thinking and actions. You are providing such a tremendously powerful and valuable service by sharing what you have learned and showing what new problem-solving skills look like in action.* I have lost count of the number of times I have witnessed evidence and insights initiating a shift in how leaders support their staff. I have seen even the most "stuck in status quo" professionals begin to use these new skills, and how new insights provide hope and inspiration across the organization, signaling that learning is valued and appreciated.

Beyond using the PAUSE framework to accomplish inspiring problem-solving, you can also apply the learning you gain to your success in grant writing and relationship building. Grant applications often look like a set of wishful promises. Can you imagine how much more powerful and potentially convincing it would be if you wrote a grant that said, "We recently interviewed X stakeholders to learn about their greatest needs. These are their greatest pain points. Here's our idea for how to address the key challenge; here are all of the most important unknowns and assumptions that could get in the way [which the funder is probably already thinking about]; here's how we tested them; and here are our early results that demonstrate impact." Wowee! Information like this would knock their socks off compared to the "once upon a time" (promise of impact) content most funders weed through. I've heard funders say that if an application like this were submitted, it would stand head and shoulders above the rest, and it would be foolish not to fund it.

The same packaging of your learning holds true with potential donors, as well as partners, board members, and the community. By using the PAUSE framework, you are exhibiting your values in action. Sharing your learning conveys the confident message that you invest your resources in solutions that are codesigned and validated by stakeholders to create the deepest impact.

## What Else Do You Still Need to Learn?

Just as you are never done with empathy, you are absolutely never done learning. There are many paths that this new leg of your learning journey can take, and you truly need to follow the evidence. While you are on your learning journey, you will pick up on the nuances of the different types of value you create for different stakeholders. Once you have validated the needs of one group, you'll want to see if other stakeholders have similar needs and obstacles, and if the potential solution will work for them as well, perhaps with some adjustments. The learning paths can feel winding, but ultimately, they are significant timesavers. As you use the PAUSE framework to work through each stakeholder group, you quickly get a 360-degree view of the challenge from multiple perspectives, and you can then codesign ways to create value for multiple stakeholders at once. As new challenges pop up, you apply the very same five skills to remove uncertainty and drive your decisions with data and insights.

If you are reading this and thinking, "I don't have *time* to learn this way," I encourage you to trust the process, stay the course, and remember the amazing insights you had with just a handful of interviews and tests. Working with the PAUSE framework is so much more effective and efficient than our typical "giant triangles of waste," but you need to commit to working differently and follow the learning to see the benefits.

## Getting to Implementation

You might also be thinking, "So I run a bunch of tests until I feel confident about my solution and then I shift to execution? Is there more?" And the answer is yes, there is indeed more, but I want to be transparent about the intent of the PAUSE framework. These skills are meant to help organizations at the "noticing" or potential idea stage of exploring a challenge. The framework can be applied to nearly any area of uncertainty, including an existing or new program, process, or policy, but it was not designed to be an execution framework.

Honestly, I have not seen many organizations struggle with implementation and project management—that is what they are normally used to doing. I do, however, see an opportunity to use people's superpowers where they can create the biggest impact. Just as I talked about "search" and "execution" challenges, I believe there are "search" and "execution" people. There are people who love to think big, challenge thinking, and dissect systems, and they need the freedom to explore. There are also people for whom one plus one must always equal two, and who love guidelines, timelines, project flows, and fine detail.

Although it is very powerful to have a combination of "search" and "execution" people on a team (some people fall also somewhere in between), it can be useful to let loose your "search," wide-open, "what could be possible if…?" thinkers so they can focus on empathy and testing solutions, and your "execution," "how will we put this into action?" rock stars to focus on how they can bring your validated solution to reality. If you are laughing because you are a team of one or have a tiny team who has to be all-skilled and wear all the hats, you should still consider what type of work you most enjoy and where you can put your superpowers into action.

That said, the PAUSE framework absolutely applies to execution. Let's say you feel confident about putting your solution into action; it can be very helpful to consider uncertainties embedded within the implementation. Think about some of the unknowns that still might be lingering with regard to the stages of execution:

- Who will be responsible for the project and why?

- How, when, and by whom will the solution be introduced to new stakeholders?

- What additional resources or materials are needed to implement the solution?

- What do leaders need to do to provide their full support?

Each of these uncertainties is connected to internal or external stakeholders whom you can interview and with whom you can codesign potential implementation strategies. You can't do all of this delicious work rooted in empathy, and identifying your own assumptions, and then ignore the needs of your colleagues or assume that they can work miracles or have all of the resources necessary to help bring the solution to life. This is why the two questions you learned in Assess Uncertainty—"What do I know for sure?" and "What do I still need to learn?"—are so powerful and should be continually asked, even in implementation work. If you keep those questions top of mind, you will start to have little alarm bells go off when you encounter uncertainty, and now you know what skills to apply to advance your learning and guide your next steps!

## Final Thoughts

Wow! What a journey you have been on! Whether you have only read through the content, paused at each stage to apply the activities to your work (or even with a team), thoughtfully paused to consider the questions at the end of each chapter, or perhaps a mix of all of those, well done, you! I am proud and appreciative of you as a reader and changemaker and of your dedication to considering and using the PAUSE skills.

**P:** Package the Challenge
**A:** Assess Uncertainty
**U:** Understand Stakeholders
**S:** Solution Testing
**E:** Evidence-Informed Decision-Making

I hope that you use these skills whenever you experience uncertainty, and that, instead of creating "giant triangles of waste," you consider how you can work differently (*and more successfully*) to

- write your next grant application,
- form your next coalition,
- design your next program,
- begin strategic planning, and
- pursue "change management" approaches.

I'm assuming that you too are a frustrated changemaker like me and that you want to create a positive impact in your organization and community and contribute to change across the sector. You want your teams and partners to do their very best work. You care about doing good, about it feeling good, and about it actually making a difference.

You can choose to be visionary, join a community of next-level changemakers, and get results beyond what you've ever experienced. By working differently, you can make real, lasting change *and* feel inspired, confident, excited, and connected to your purpose.

*You* can

- be the one to shift how you create change inside and outside your organization,

- shape a work environment where people are invigorated and inspired,

- use data and learning to guide your work and influence decision-makers,

- invest in skills that will serve you immediately and into the future, and

- authentically connect with your community and cocreate solutions that you know will work.

The PAUSE skills are intended to help you address uncertainty and drive greater impact while saving time and money. I created this framework not only to make sense of how we do our work in the social impact sector—in nonprofit, local government, and philanthropy—but to challenge and change the way we change the world.

I'm not going to tell you that addressing challenges using this framework will always be an easy or simple journey (and that is partly why I started this book with a "Dear Frustrated Changemaker" love note), but it is time for us to collectively change our mindsets, practices, and what we make possible. It's time to create new outcomes, and I know we can. People just like you can use new skills and strategies that fit *this* time of growing uncertainty to create a new future for the sector and our world.

## PAUSE AND CONSIDER

TO BE alive is to learn. Life is all about being curious, traveling new paths, sharing with others, and making choices. You have been on an amazing learning journey applying the PAUSE framework to your work and uncertainty. And you know what? You're not done, and you never will be. We are not done because we are continually evolving to meet the ever-shifting needs and uncertainties impacting our sector, organizations, and communities. Consider these questions:

- How do you share information with decision-makers?

- While you are learning about one area of uncertainty, what do you do when something else pops up that is also uncertain? Is it documented, shared, and explored?

- Think about yourself and others on your team or in your organization. Can you think of who might be considered "search" and "execution" people? What characteristics do they exhibit that make you think they fit into these categories?

- When you execute an idea, do you identify the unknowns and assumptions connected to making the idea a reality?

- Now that you've learned about all of the PAUSE skills, which skill resonates most? Do you have a favorite?

- What do you want to accomplish and how do you want to impact your organization and community?

# 16

# Dear Leaders

I BEGAN THIS book with a letter to all the frustrated change-makers. Now I want to leave a few words for leaders (and yes, you might be frustrated changemakers too).

Leaders, I'll be honest: I've had some tricky relationships with you. I have worked with many leaders in very diverse organizations tackling very diverse challenges. At times, you inspire me and make me believe that anything is possible. Other times, you frustrate and disappoint me beyond measure. I can hold the tension between your greatness and your weakness, but honestly, I care about this work because I care about stakeholders. Whether internal or external, they deserve the very best of you and what you can make possible.

You are key to the sector, your community, your organization, and your staff, shifting to create deeper and more positive impact.

When you PAUSE, not only do you wisely invest your resources and eliminate waste, but you also have the power to

- guide your culture;
- inspire, empower, and engage your staff (while also improving staff recruitment and retention);

- create amazing programs, policies, and processes;

- not just support but also delight stakeholders;

- create strong and effective collaborations; and

- generate new revenue and funding support.

I have seen amazing leaders accomplish these tasks using the PAUSE framework, and the very best leaders who access the full potential and power of these new problem-solving skills have a few common traits.

**Leaders listen.** You absorb and integrate learning without judgment.

**Leaders show up.** You physically show up (undistracted) to hear updates, and you provide your full support and resources to remove obstacles and provide access to learning.

**Leaders appreciate.** You tell individuals and teams who work this way how proud, impressed, and full of gratitude you are for all of the learning they have contributed to the organization.

**Leaders communicate.** You tell others in the organization what has been learned and create opportunities for other stakeholders to learn and ask questions.

**Leaders act.** You take the learning and apply it. You respect the evidence and make decisions that move validated projects to execution and dismiss projects for which the data show weak impact.

**Leaders ripple.** You commit to more, see additional uncertainty to address, begin to integrate the skills, and create learning pathways for others to acquire and practice these skills.

**Leaders mentor.** You commit to being a guardian and cheer-leader of the process and learning. This is not the time for heavy management and rigid parameters. When you're in uncertainty, ditch expectations of how, by when, and the potential outcomes, and focus on the learning journey.

In addition to the leadership traits that help organizations thrive and shine, there are five core wishes that internal staff whom I've had the honor to support consistently want from their leaders. Staff want to

1 know that you support them;

2 be seen as valued key stakeholders;

3 understand what is going on—they need communication, clarity, and transparency;

4 know the "North Star" of the organization and how their work relates; and

5 see you walk the talk—they are watching what you do ver-sus what you say.

When staff are excited about using the PAUSE skills, there are five obstacles leaders can unintentionally create or perpet-uate that stand in the way of learning.

**Fear of "failure":** Even when leaders say they "support learn-ing," staff are usually skeptical and fearful of presenting evidence that goes against accepted norms or expected out-comes. They need to experience the freedom and positive reinforcement for learning new information, and it is essen-tial that leaders reinforce the assurance that all outcomes and learning are considered successes.

**Not everyone is on board:** Often, there is an unequal distribution of power and support for new strategies across the entire
organization. A top leader can say, "We are using the PAUSE
framework and working in new ways," and they might get a
basic level of buy-in from some staff, while others in the organization can delay, derail, or demoralize staff and teams who
try to work differently. I have seen this most often with middle
managers who see change as another thing they must man-
age. Leaders must closely watch these dynamics and build
expectations for learning and the adoption of skills into the
accountability metrics of everyone's job performance.

**Change theater is easier than real change:** This is one of
the most soul-crushing and difficult issues to encounter and
confront. A leader will say they want change and to be future-
forward and visionary—they even read "all the books"—and
people believe them (myself included). Unfortunately, when
it's time for action, some leaders reveal that they were just
posturing, they were just satisfying their itch for another
bright shiny object, and they go back to work as usual. Sometimes this shows up as weak leadership support. Other times,
once leaders see early evidence of a potential solution or a
new idea to address a different challenge, they ask teams to
jump into full execution mode, right back into "giant triangle"
status quo problem-solving, ignoring additional uncertainties
and assumptions to be tested.

Using the PAUSE skills can also be a test of a leader's style:
I think some leaders realize (although it may not be outwardly
expressed) that while they thought they could be open to new
ideas and sharing power, they actually prefer to have more
power and control, and they regress to more comfortable
"best practice" solutions and top-down decision-making.

I have the most difficult time absorbing change theater
because it can be highly destructive. Staff experience the

transformation that the framework creates, and it can be extremely frustrating and deflating to return to status quo problem-solving after they've felt the difference. In these instances, I have seen staff members leave their organizations (which is never, ever my intent) because seeing the power of the new skills and new learning ignored is the last straw. I do my very best to identify potential "change theatrics" so that I do not work with leaders who might put staff in those awful situations, and I try to gracefully and effectively navigate these dynamics if they do appear.

**No time, resources, or room on the plate:** Leaders will get excited by the tremendous insights teams gain, and they say they want to keep pushing the solution forward to execution and continue to work this way, while at the same time providing no time or space for staff to integrate extra time and energy into their schedules. This is a bit different from the scenario above because the leader continues to champion and proselytize this way of working but unfortunately does not provide ways to integrate the work. This work does not have to be overly time-consuming—progress can be made in just a matter of hours over several weeks—but it does need to be prioritized and supported.

**Silos:** Even while teams might be formed across departments, silos, and hierarchies, and make great progress on a challenge and improve information sharing and relationship building, the rest of the organization remains fractured. These disconnects make sharing information and resources to move potential solutions to execution very difficult and can kill momentum for applying the skills to additional challenges.

I totally understand that addressing these traits and tasks can feel difficult and overwhelming, especially when you have very difficult jobs. As leaders, you have so many pushes and pulls, layers of complexity, and professional and personal goals and challenges you are balancing, most of which no one knows anything about. You are managing your own imposter syndrome, finding clarity in next steps, and navigating constant uncertainty, and all while you are expected to have the answers to everything. You deserve empathy too, because many people don't know what it is to walk in your shoes.

That said, leaders, you can also know better and do better. There are some specific changes you can make to elevate your impact internally and externally.

**Work on culture.** Both a negative and positive organizational culture will ripple out and, bad and good, there will be consequences and opportunities. Culture impacts every element of your daily and larger strategic tasks and goals. Many leaders often wait for their culture to emerge (for newer organizations), think that staff should create or shape it, or put it last on the priority list. Since culture touches every element of your work, it needs to be a top and consistent priority.

**Work on yourself.** This is true for all of us, even if you think you are one of the "good ones." The very best leaders are vulnerable, self-aware, empathetic, active listeners, and engaged learners. Like anyone else, you hold organizational and personal trauma, and you are on your own learning journey. It is essential that you find ways to nurture and seek support for developing and growing all these skills.

**Follow the evidence.** Commit to empowering data and insights, not pet projects or what you think should work, to guide your decision-making. Hold yourself and other powerholders accountable for testing ideas before you implement them.

Change requires learning, not change management. So many leaders and organizations have bought into the idea that leaders "solve" the problem, decide the direction, shape the messaging, and enforce expectations of how others will fall into line. Relying just on change management strategies for big shifts rarely works well or smoothly.

You can use the PAUSE framework to explore and test changes before you go to full scale. Just as you often don't know exactly which solutions are going to create the greatest impact for stakeholders, you also don't know what's going to best help integrate big changes into your existing culture. You can use the PAUSE framework to address the embedded layers of uncertainty and assumptions, and codesign potential strategies with internal stakeholders, in turn creating empathetic connections and shared power.

**Act differently.** Most people are watching and judging your actions. People might listen to what you say, but what they are really often waiting and watching for is what you will do. They want to see if you'll do what you said you would and if your actions will match your words. There is unfortunately a large disconnect sometimes between saying and doing, and it takes awareness, commitment, and hard work to be in alignment.

I share this learning from a decade of working with leaders not to scare you away, or for you to interpret this learning as some sort of checklist for how you need to prepare, be perfect, or be "ready" to use the PAUSE framework. I share this information because I care deeply about you, your staff, your organization, your community, and our sector.

You might ask, "So, how do I get started?" The answer is to use the PAUSE framework. I tell leaders all the time to use the framework to roll out the framework. You may never have introduced a new learning and problem-solving strategy across your organization. To do something new and across the organization sounds highly uncertain with many embedded unknowns and assumptions, and that is what the framework was made for!

To figure out how to most effectively and efficiently lead new ways of working to create more impact, leaders often identify one challenge and one team to begin their journey. It is so informative for me to watch an organization and team in action as they learn and use the skills. I get to see how leaders and staff show up, and I get signals about the organization's culture and ability to learn. Organizations usually will extend their work to tackle additional challenges and train more staff, sometimes forming their own internal team of coaches via a train-the-trainer model that then guides future initiatives. I honestly apply the PAUSE skills myself (especially those connected to empathy and assumptions) to shape the support that I provide, as I too am on a learning journey with each and every client.

The PAUSE framework is not magic, but a *process (and a practice)*. No one enjoys uncertainty, and leading an organization through the unknown requires numerous skills. There is no perfect time to learn, engage your staff, create deeper impact, and prevent waste from using status quo problem-solving skills. You just have to get started and trust the process.

# Acknowledgments

HAVE A quote on my desk that says, "What writes us as we write it," and I've let this book write me. The process of being so intentional and thoughtful about how I share my learning and my words has been transformative. I am most blessed to know the beautiful humans who have supported me and whom I have encountered on this journey. I want to first thank those people who have been most intimately involved in this incubation and "birthing" process.

My partner, Jon, has witnessed and supported me through all the feels, from the excited, "shake my booty" celebrations to the exhausted "can/should I really do this" moments. He is my true "home" and he continuously roots me in love, possibility, and the fullness of life.

My kiddos keep me grounded in the struggle and beauty of the mundane (think school drop-offs, grocery shopping—you know, life, life). They remind me that my work and this book are just artifacts of my journey, but it is they who make my journey sweet.

Thanks to my mom and sister, who have shaped the person I choose to be today but also continue to support me even when they don't really understand what I do.

The team at Page Two has been phenomenal to work with and abundantly kind. I have loved working with Jesse

Finkelstein, cofounder of the company and a fierce supporter of me and this book. I have thought about writing this book for years, and after I sent Jesse the first thirty pages, she became focused on making it happen. Emily Schultz, my amazing editor, truly supported me through the emotional and evolving processes that are adding, clarifying, and trimming. Steph VanderMeulen, whom I refer to as my "nitty-gritty" copyeditor, has examined every single character of this book, which I'm in awe of and for which I feel deep appreciation. Adrineh Der-Boghossian, my project manager, is the epitome of patience, clarity, and encouragement. Chris Brandt has guided my thinking about marketing and all the ways in which I can support frustrated changemakers, and Taysia Louie, who designed the cover and interior elements of the book, nailed them on her first tries.

So many beautiful people who happen to be authors have guided me so lovingly and with such vulnerability in this process, and I want to specifically thank Amy J. Wilson, Rob Volpe, Dr. Anita Nowak, and Maria Ross (who introduced me to Jesse!). Many others have answered my numerous questions and shared their publishing journeys, and you all gave me the confidence to know that I could do this. Special thanks to Becky Pallack, who wrote the best comments on my first, very rough draft and has remained my steadfast friend and motivator.

To Amelia Klawon, my former cofounder of multiple ventures and one of the best humans ever: I want to express my deep appreciation and acknowledgment for what we envisioned and created together. Our learning and work made this book possible, and I treasure how your support and superpowers helped me grow in every way.

I want to thank all of the clients who have trusted the process and whose stories have been featured in this book and in other formats. You have invested in not only me but also this work, which now benefits so many others.

Huge thanks to the following lovely individuals who, with more than fifty others, contributed financial support via Kickstarter to bring this book to life: Kristin Hatch and Delaina Miller, John Hatch, Dr. Raquel Gutierrez, and Eduardo F. Ortiz. Thank you for believing in me and this work, and for your very generous gifts.

I also want to acknowledge some people who continually influence my thinking, many of whom are cited in this book. I share so much gratitude for the inspiration of Rachel Ramjattan, Vu Le, Darryl Lester, George Aye, Rachael Dietkus, Edgar Villanueva, Dr. Lesley-Ann Noel, Dr. Lakeya Cherry, Tania Anaissie, Alvin Schexnider, Dr. Raquel Gutierrez, Hilary Sedovic, Nate Wong, Michael O'Bryan, and many others.

A big thank you to you, the reader, for pausing to consider and reimagine what is possible.

I want to leave you with this excerpt from Octavia E. Butler's *Parable of the Sower* to guide your journey.

**All that you touch**
**You Change.**

**All that you Change**
**Changes you.**

**The only lasting truth**
**Is Change.**

**God**
**Is Change.**

I hope that you are changed on your learning journey and that you continue to seek new and better ways to change the way *we* change the world.

# Notes

## 2: The Tension between Loving and Hating the Sector

*and what Dr. Ibram X. Kendi calls "Savior Theology":* Dr. Ibram X. Kendi (@drIbram), "The White savior idea is literally 567 years old, at least. It is so deeply held, so widespread, no wonder there was such a visceral and angry reaction to my challenging that racist idea; my challenging the fallacy that the White savior is 'not racist,'" Twitter, September 27, 2020, 3:50 p.m., twitter.com/dribram/status/131030 5864939704320.

*I use the terms "lived" and "living experience":* See creativereactionlab.com/ trainings-workshops.

*I love the model of community cultural wealth:* Tara J. Yosso, "Whose Culture Has Capital? A Critical Race Theory Discussion of Community Cultural Wealth," *Race Ethnicity and Education*, Routledge, 8, no. 1 (2005), tandfonline.com/doi/abs/10.1080/13613 32052000341006.

*A habit loop begins with a cue:* "How Habits Work," Charles Duhigg (website), accessed October 19, 2022, https://charlesduhigg.com/ how-habits-work/.

## 3: Our Desire to Take Action Creates Waste at Scale

*white dominant culture's focus on "one right way":* Tema Okun, White Supremacy Culture (website), accessed October 19, 2022, https://www.whitesupremacyculture.info.

## 5: What Do We Do Instead?

*But as Brené Brown aptly shares:* Helen Walters: "Vulnerability Is the
Birthplace of Innovation, Creativity and Change: Brené Brown at
TED2012," TED Blog, March 2, 2012, blog.ted.com/vulnerability-is
-the-birthplace-of-innovation-creativity-and-change-brene-brown
-at-ted2012.

*Amy Edmondson, Harvard Business School professor:* See Edmonson's
website, amycedmondson.com, for her books, blog, and resources
on the Learning Zone.

## 8: Assess Uncertainty

*Consider Shunryu Suzuki's words:* Shunryu Suzuki, *Zen Mind, Beginner's
Mind: Informal Talks on Zen Meditation and Practice* (Boston and
London: Shambhala, 2006).

*In case you are under the illusion that you are not biased:* This is Wikipedia's
complete (as of 2016) list of cognitive biases, arranged and designed
by John Manoogian III (jm3). Categories and descriptions originally
by Buster Benson, "Cognitive Bias Codex," Wikimedia Commons,
commons.wikimedia.org/wiki/File:The_Cognitive_Bias_Codex_
-_180%2B_biases,_designed_by_John_Manoogian_III_(jm3).png; see
also Buster Benson, "Cognitive Biases," busterbenson.com/piles/
cognitive-biases.

*As Kerry Edelstein, founder of Research Narrative states:* Kerry Edelstein,
"So, You're Like a Freelancer?" Research Narrative, February 28, 2018,
researchnarrative.com/thinkerry/so-youre-like-a-freelancer.

*The Ladder of Inference shows how our brains process:* The Ladder of
Inference was developed by Chris Argyris, a former professor at
Harvard Business School, in 1970. In 1990, the Ladder of Inference
became popular after being described in the bestseller *The Fifth
Discipline: The Art & Practice of The Learning Organization* (New York:
Penguin Random House, 1990), which Argyris wrote in collaboration
with American scientist Peter M. Senge.

## 9: Understand Stakeholders

*In an excellent article:* Ovetta Sampson, "Stop Bastardizing Design with
False Empathy," *Medium,* December 30, 2020, medium.com/swlh/
stop-bastardizing-design-with-false-empathy-6a06d431bab3.

*Sampson discusses the work:* Daniel Goleman, *Emotional Intelligence:
The Groundbreaking Book that Redefines What It Means to Be Smart*
(New York: Bantam Books, 2020).

*Brené Brown has a well-known YouTube video:* Brené Brown, "Brené Brown on Empathy," YouTube video, 2:53, youtube.com/watch?v=1Evwgu 369Jw.

*Consider this statement:* Sampson, "Stop Bastardizing Design with False Empathy."

*As George Aye ... astutely points out:* George Aye, "That Quiet Little Voice," presented at Fortune Brainstorm Design conference, May 2022, Greater Good Studio, Vimeo video, 19:48, vimeo.com/716028267.

*My thinking about consent:* Tad Hirsch, "Practicing Without a License: Design Research as Psychotherapy," in *CHI '20: Proceedings of the 2020 CHI Conference on Human Factors in Computing Systems*, 1-11 (New York: Association for Computing Machinery), published online April 23, 2020, doi.org/10.1145/3313831.3376750.

*Rachael has informed much of my thinking:* Rachael Dietkus, "A Transdisciplinary Model of Change for Trauma Responsive Design Research," Social Workers Who Design, 2021, socialworkerswho .design/modelofchange.

## 10: Gaining Insights into People's Actions

*I'll leave you once more with the words:* Sampson, "Stop Bastardizing Design with False Empathy."

## 12: Solution Testing

*American actor Alan Alda once said:* Alan Alda, "62nd Commencement Address," *Commencement Addresses*, Paper 7, June 1, 1980, Digital Commons @ Connecticut College, digitalcommons.conncoll.edu/ commence/7.

## Acknowledgments

*I want to leave you with this excerpt:* Octavia E. Butler, *Parable of the Sower* (New York: Grand Central Publishing, 2019).

# How I Can Help

KNOW THAT when I read books, I sometimes put the authors on a pedestal and think, "They are the *author* (ooh la la); I can't reach out to *them*." I share this because I am so not "ooh la la," and I want you to reach out! I want to hear your questions, concerns, and ideas, and how you want to reimagine the sector. I really love connecting with others, so please don't be shy. Send me an email at heather@pauseforchange.com.

I truly enjoy helping social impact organizations (nonprofit, local government, philanthropy) address uncertainty in less time and using fewer resources to achieve greater impact.

Amazing people and organizations just like you and yours

- hire me to train and lead their teams to address internal or external challenges,

- take my online courses to learn how to apply the PAUSE skills to their own work,

- invite me to keynote and lead workshops at conferences and events, and

- sign up for my newsletter and learn golden nuggets as I gather them.

You can learn about all of this goodness and more at PauseforChange.com and follow my latest learning and opportunities on LinkedIn (linkedin.com/in/heatherhiscox).

As I shared, there is also so much content that did not make it into this book but that I would love for you to access to learn more and receive additional support. Go to my book website, NoMoreStatusQuoBook.com, to download the articles, tools, and other resources.

I truly appreciate you and the energy you dedicated to reading this book and, hopefully, applying the PAUSE skills to your work. I'm here to help and would love to meet you, so please connect!

NIEVES MONTAÑO

# About the Author

HEATHER HISCOX is a #FrustratedChangemaker on a mission to change the way we change the world. Heather is the founder and CEO of Pause for Change. The PAUSE method is a proven and proprietary framework that helps changemakers address difficult challenges and pursue promising opportunities. These skills help organizations be certain about which solutions will create the greatest impact while using fewer resources and less time. Heather is also the cocreator and host of Possibility Project (www.possibilityproject.org), an online conversion series and growing community of disruptive changemakers reclaiming their power through meaningful sparks, connections, and action. Heather speaks at conferences and events about social impact (nonprofit, local government, and philanthropic) disruption and innovation, and has launched several ventures that benefit the social impact sector, connecting organizations to the training, skills, and resources they need to deepen their impact.

Lightning Source UK Ltd.
Milton Keynes UK
UKHW012048060223
416584UK00007B/199